A London Design Studio 1880–1963 **The Silver Studio Collection**

Diana Dolman

DESIGNED
BY J & R SILVER

A London Design Studio 1880–1963

The Silver Studio Collection

Foreword by John Brandon-Jones

Introduction by Mark Turner

With a contribution by William Ruddick

Lund Humphries · London

in association with the Middlesex Polytechnic

First edition 1980
Published by
Lund Humphries Publishers Ltd
26 Litchfield Street London WC2

SBN 85331 431 4

Designed by Herbert Spencer
Filmset by Keyspools Ltd, Golborne, Lancs.
Printed and bound by Lund Humphries, Bradford, Yorks.

Photography by Tony Saunders and John Morgan

Cover illustrations:
front: 104(b); back: 205

This is the catalogue of the exhibition 'A London Design Studio 1880–1963: The Silver Studio Collection' held at the Museum of London from 21 November 1980 to 31 January 1981 and subsequently at Wolverhampton Art Gallery from 21 February to 28 March 1981; at Bradford Art Galleries and Museums from 11 April to 7 June 1981; and at Laing Art Gallery, Newcastle-upon-Tyne from 20 June to 26 July 1981

Contents

Arthur Silver 1853–1896

Foreword

by John Brandon-Jones

The last two decades of the nineteenth century saw a remarkable upsurge in the quality of decorative art in Britain. William Morris was active and the names of designers of the calibre of Mackmurdo, Voysey and Mackintosh are familiar to everyone interested in the applied arts. Their reputations are safe, their designs have frequently been exhibited and discussed at length in many recently published books and periodicals.

The name of Arthur Silver, on the other hand, is probably known only to a few of those who have made a special study of the period but he and his associates made an outstanding contribution as designers in many fields from 1880 onwards. Moreover, the Studio he founded continued to produce important work under his son, Rex Silver, until it was wound up in 1963.

Fortunately the records of the Silver Studio have been preserved; they are now in the care of the Middlesex Polytechnic, and the present exhibition displays a selection of the work produced over the whole period of the firm's existence.

Only a small proportion of the total output of the Studio actually appeared over the name of Silver because the designs were sold to manufacturers and specialist shops such as Liberty's, who preferred to use their own brand names and kept the names of the actual designers to themselves. Students of architectural history have always known that a number of great reputations have, in reality, depended upon the work of anonymous draughtsmen, known in the profession as 'Ghosts'. In the Silver Studio Exhibition we can, at last, see the work of one of the greatest Ghost organisations ever to work in the field of applied art.

The versatility of the members of the Silver Studio was extraordinary. At the drop of a hat they could produce designs for textiles or metalwork, book jackets or complete schemes for interior decoration. Every type of commission came as grist to the Silver mill and, unlike the prima donnas of the profession, they were happy to design in 'period' as well as in the 'contemporary' styles. It is fascinating to follow, in the work of a single firm, the twists and turns of fashion over a period of eighty years.

Acknowledgements

Design history is a comparatively recent area of academic study which is coming increasingly to the fore in universities and polytechnics at both undergraduate and postgraduate levels. At Middlesex Polytechnic the Silver Studio Collection will play an important part in design history research, and with this in mind, we decided to organise an exhibition for 1980 which would both publicise the collection and celebrate the centenary of the founding of the Silver Studio.

Our very greatest thanks are due to Miss Mary Peerless (Rex Silver's step daughter) who not only donated the collection in the first place but has since given tirelessly of her advice and time in its subsequent management and in the preparation of this exhibition. Other members of the family have given invaluable assistance in this exhibition. We would particularly like to thank Mrs Erica Haxworth for not only providing much information on her father, Harry Silver, but for generously lending objects designed by him. Her sister, Mrs Gay Silver, has lent a christening set from a design by her father. Miss Barbara Sturgis has provided considerable information on her mother, the actress Christine Silver and on her uncle, Rex Silver, and grandfather, Arthur Silver. Appropriately, the exhibition has been superbly designed by Arthur Silver's great grandson, Mr Martyn Haxworth, assisted by Mr Jay Stewart and Mr Bob Carter.

One of the hardest tasks connected with this exhibition was the tracing of designers who worked at the Studio. It was therefore particularly gratifying to hear from Miss Winifred Mold, who worked at the Silver Studio from 1912 until 1935, and who very kindly provided much information about the Studio and its working methods. We are also indebted to Mr Neil Illingworth Kay for information on his father, Mr John Illingworth Kay, and for lending paintings and objects by him. Mrs Eunice Wright has taken much trouble to visit the collection and to provide very useful information about her father, Frank Price, who was the last full-time member of staff at the Studio.

We are very grateful to Mr John Brandon-Jones for kindly providing a foreword to the catalogue, and to Mr William Ruddick for his scholarly article on the Silver Family.

This exhibition has been made possible by generous donations from The Arts Council of Great Britain, The South East Area Museums Service, The Worshipful Company of Goldsmiths, Sotheby & Co., and Reed International.

Members of staff of a number of institutions have provided considerable assistance with the preparation of this exhibition. We would particularly like to thank Mrs Barbara Morris, formerly of the Victoria and Albert Museum and now with Sotheby & Co., for her constant involvement with the collection and for giving so generously of her advice and knowledge. At the Victoria and Albert Museum, Mrs Shirley Bury has provided much scholarly information on the cataloguing of the Silver Studio's metalwork designs and Mrs Valerie Mendes and Mrs Linda Parry, both of the Textile Department, have kindly provided information on the textiles in the collection and organised the loan of objects from their department. We would also like to thank Miss Hester Bury of Warner & Sons Ltd for information on the Silver Studio's work for her firm, and for the loan of textiles and designs to this exhibition.

The textile conservation for the exhibition has been superbly organised and executed by Mrs June Marshall, with the assistance of volunteers, mostly from the Harrow branch of the National Association of Decorative and Fine Arts Societies. These include Mrs Mavis Starns, Mrs Mary Alloway, Mrs Janet Phillips, Mrs Muriel Rata, Mrs Gladys Jefferies, Mrs Diane Clipson, Mrs Anne O'Sullivan, Mrs Edna Rushworth and Mrs Alexander Duthie.

Within Middlesex Polytechnic, a number of members of staff have been closely involved with this exhibition. We would particularly like to thank Mr Mark Turner for his work of scholarship and artistry in selecting exhibits and writing the introduction and entries for the catalogue; Miss Sarah Mansell for splendidly skilful work in the conservation of prints, designs and wallpapers, assisted by Mrs Sheila Levy; Mrs Bobby de Joia and her staff for their enthusiastic work on the publicity and related areas for this exhibition; Ms Janice Dixon for so admirably dealing with the very large amount of secretarial work in connection with the exhibition; Mr David Cheshire for his invaluable bibliographical assistance and constant advice; and we are especially grateful to Mr Bob Hornung, Mr John Cowley and Mr Peter Green. Their tireless enthusiasm and administrative support have made this exhibition possible.

Finally, we would like to thank warmly Lund Humphries Publishers Ltd, and in particular Mr John Taylor, for having been such valued colleagues in the production of this catalogue.

The Silver Studio Steering Committee
Middlesex Polytechnic
Bounds Green Road
London N11

January 1980

Lenders to the Exhibition

Mr and Mrs Alexander Duthie
Mr Peter Haxworth
Mr and Mrs William Haxworth
Mr and Mrs Neil Illingworth Kay
Miss Mary Peerless
Mr and Mrs Silver
The Victoria and Albert Museum
Warner and Sons Ltd

Introduction

by Mark Turner

In 1967, through the generosity of Miss Mary Peerless, the contents of the Silver Studio of Design were presented to Hornsey College of Art, which is now part of Middlesex Polytechnic. As a result of this gift, the Polytechnic possesses a unique archive and research library and one of the most comprehensive collections of decorative design material in the country. As a research collection, its importance is very great. The Silver Studio at all times kept meticulous records, so that it is possible to date almost all of the 20,000 designs now in the collection. By using the surviving day books and diaries, it is often possible to attribute both designer and purchaser for any given design. In conjunction with the written records there is also a photographic archive of nearly all sold designs which runs from c.1890 to 1963 and which is cross-referenced to the design and day-book numbers.

In all, the collection comprises about 20,000 designs, 2,000 wallpapers, 50 wallpaper pattern books, about 4,000 textile samples, a large library of works on design and related subjects, a collection of visual reference material and approximately 4,000 postcards, letters, trade cards, newspaper cuttings and miscellanea.

The Silver Studio was directed by Arthur and Rex Silver, who were father and son. Arthur Silver (1853–96) ran the Studio from 84 Brook Green, Hammersmith, then 4 Haarlem Road, later giving up No. 4 and buying No. 3 Haarlem Road, directly behind 84 Brook Green. Rex Silver (1879–1965) ran the Studio from 1901 to 1963 (in partnership with his younger brother, Harry, until 1916). In 1912, Rex sold No.3 Haarlem Road and bought the Corner House, No.1, Haarlem Road, where the Studio remained until Rex Silver's death.

The Silver Studio between 1880 and 1963 produced nearly 30,000 designs, mostly for furnishing textiles and wallpapers, but also for complete interiors, plasterwork, dress fabrics, stencils, metalwork, furniture, book jackets, advertisements and trade cards. They designed for an enormous range of manufacturers who provided for all classes of society.

This exhibition has two aims – to present an accurate account of English decorative design history over the period of the Studio's operation, and to publicise the work of Arthur, Rex and Harry Silver and the designers who worked for them, whose output, in the normal course of events, would have gone largely unrecognised.

Arthur Silver was born in Reading in 1853. His grandfather is recorded as having a cabinet-making business in Reading in 1837 and his father, James Silver, described himself in the Reading Trade Directory of 1865 as an 'Upholsterer, cabinet maker, paper hanger, estate agent, valuer, undertaker and agent to the Eagle Life Office'.[1] Although nothing is known of Arthur's childhood, he could hardly have been brought up in a more propitious atmosphere, where he would have had the opportunity to become familiar with furnishing textiles and wallpapers. Most furnishing textiles in the 1860s were woven – velvets, brocades and damask, and this may partly explain Arthur's great ability to design for these materials. An early interest in design can be assumed because in 1869 he attended Reading School of Art. This was one of the many schools of art established by Sir Henry Cole in an attempt to train a generation of designers who would satisfactorily unite art with industry. In fact the impetus for the stylistic innovations of the 1880s and 1890s came from designers with an architectural background rather than from former art school pupils. There is some evidence to suggest that design was not particularly well taught at these schools. Robert Edis complained: 'I cannot see why it is necessary to make students work continuously upon designs of repeated geometric forms – in which there is an absence of all artistic feeling – which are called ornamental. . . . All this is machinery work of the hand and loses all trace of human mind or thought'.[2] One of the few remaining records of Arthur's period at Reading School of Art is a page in a sketch book dated 1872 of very carefully drawn geometric patterns copied from Owen Jones's *Grammar of Ornament*.

Arthur Silver's career at Reading seems to have been both uneventful and moderately successful. In 1870 he was awarded a copy of *Half Hour Lectures on the History and Practice of the Fine and Ornamental Arts* by William Bell Scott (who had himself been Headmaster of the Government School of Art at Newcastle-upon-Tyne) for success in the elementary section of the course of Introduction in Art. A certificate recording his proficiency in the Freehand Drawing and Perspective Exercises in the Second Grade Examination on 6 May 1870 also exists. On 24 May 1872 his performance in the Geometrical Exercise in the Second Grade Examination was judged 'Excellent'. His certificate recording a second class pass in the Vegetable Anatomy and Physiology examination ten days earlier bears a copy of the signature of Sir Henry Cole.

On leaving Reading School of Art in 1872 Arthur Silver had the great fortune to be apprenticed to the talented and progressive designer, H.W. Batley. Batley's work charts very well the various movements in design that occurred between 1860 and 1900. He himself wrote in 1882:[3] 'The Gothic Revival of some years back, although very sound and good in its way, was soon found to be too heavy and severe for domestic use . . .'. Alexander Millar wrote of him in *Design for Modern Carpets*:[4] 'While the so-called Early English style was in vogue, it was very sucessfully adapted to carpets by Mr H.W.Batley.' By 1873, when Arthur Silver became his apprentice, he had abandoned Gothic and was working in a number of different styles for furniture, textiles and wallpapers, and the surviving sketch books and designs by Arthur from the 1870s show that Batley had successfully taught him how to work in these (see 39, 51). They range from heavy naturalistic flower designs for textiles and wallpapers, derived from the French Second Empire style, to elegant Queen Anne Revival furniture designs. Batley often used Japanese motifs in his furniture designs in the 1870s and it would seem likely that Arthur Silver first acquired a knowledge of Japanese art from him. Batley also had contacts with most of the leading wallpaper and textile manufacturers of the day, and a sound practical knowledge of the technicalities involved in designing for specific materials. All this was to be of the greatest benefit to Arthur's future career.

Batley remained a great friend both of Arthur Silver and his son Rex. After 1880 he concentrated more on etching than on pattern design, but in 1908, along with W.J.Paulson Townsend, Alfred Martin, Henry Poole and others, he formed the Guild of Decorators Syndicate Ltd. The Guild's catalogue states that it was[5] 'Founded in the belief that Art is not degraded, but rather ennobled by its closest association with commerce . . .'. Attacking the more idealistic Guilds of the period, the members go on to state: 'The Guild is not a mere quixotic movement, or the expression of unpractical idealism, it is essentially a business undertaking, the management of which is in the hands of competent directors whose many years of experience in the practical side of decoration qualifies them for the position they hold.' The catalogue illustrates examples of the work of its members, including two objects designed by Batley. The first is an aesthetic-movement piano case, probably dating from c.1880, and similar to one now in the Victoria and Albert Museum. The other is a wallpaper of a much later date, in a restrained, simple Art Nouveau style, reminiscent of Voysey's wallpapers of the early 1900s. The catalogue also provides some interesting biographical information on Batley, including the fact that he was awarded the Cross of the Legion of Honour (probably for his furniture designs shown in Paris at the exhibition of 1878).

In 1878 Arthur Silver's father-in-law, W.H.Walenn had cast him a horoscope,[6] emphasising Arthur's 'continual flow of [your] own entity from within outwards. The strength and persistency of the flow is marked. But the supply of this is more than sufficient to spend itself upon daily wants and its effect upon your life is to accumulate and store itself up, as it were, for use at intervals of time upon important and worthy objects, purposes and deeds.' Prophetically, however, he warned that Arthur's projects might involve 'contest and sometimes wasted work'. It may be suspected from the existence of this document that Arthur Silver was thinking of branching out on his own in the latter years of the 1870s. In 1878 he married Isabella Walenn and they took the lease of a house at 132 Coningham Road, Shepherds Bush, West London. Their first son Rex was born in 1879, and shortly after this, in 1880, Arthur took the decisive step of opening his own studio. He could not have chosen a more propitious time. At no previous period in the nineteenth century had so many people been interested in the decoration of their houses – a fact which was fully acknowledged by relevant periodicals from *The Builder* to *Sylvia's Home Journal*. This interest was matched only by the large number of styles available in which it was possible to decorate one's house. In the 1850s and 1860s style had been of little consequence to most people. The newly-prosperous, industrious, middle-class, mid-nineteenth-century Englishman had not much time to spare for the aesthetics of interior decoration. Mrs Panton, whose books on interior decoration and household management were extremely popular in the late nineteenth century, wrote in 1919:[7] 'Fifty years ago, if carpets and curtains were bought at all, it was after high and long debates in the family, and heavens how they wore! At this moment I could put my hand on amber coloured damask curtains bought more than sixty years ago, and pieces of carpet bought more than eighty years since.' She explains that this emphasis on durability was due largely to the expense of furniture and household equipment in the 1850s and 1860s. 'I had to buy awful striped repp curtains in poisonous green, and could then only afford one stuff and one muslin curtain to each window, and naturally the stuff ones could not be drawn. . . . Bedroom ware was ugly and costly, a good deal of gilt was spread about dinner and tea sets, which in their turn took much money to replace. Wine glasses were treasures and decanters were expensive.'

Increased machine production, and competition from imported goods, led to a considerable fall in prices for most household goods in the 1880s and 1890s. In the 1850s style was of little consequence in decorating, but by 1870, England was the richest country in the world, and by 1880, Arthur Silver must have been extremely grateful to Henry Batley for having been taught to work in so many historical styles. These ranged from avant-garde aesthetic decoration, using subdued colours and Japanese motifs, to elaborate late-eighteenth-century English and French styles, French Second Empire, Moorish, Egyptian, and English Renaissance. It would seem likely that the rapid increase in the standard of living for the English middle classes meant that money, time and interest were available for interior decoration.

The eclectic clutter which replaced the heavy and monumental style of the mid-nineteenth century gave rise to a considerable amount of criticism. 'England has become a vast knick-knackery', wrote an anonymous critic in the *Saturday Review*[8] who, describing aesthetes, goes on to say: 'The beauty he loves is a beauty that springs from decay – the poetry of Baudelaire, the bronzes of Pekin, the faded graces of Madame de Pompadour. . . . In pre-Colean times rooms were adapted to the people who lived in them, but the great aim of the aesthetic friend is to make people adapt themselves to their rooms.' Another anonymous critic thought that the current interest in the design of furniture, wallpaper and textiles devalued the Fine Arts.[9] 'The theory underlying this movement . . . is what has become almost a "shibboleth" amongst art-critics of the day, that art and artistic feeling are as much shown in the design of furniture and other accessories as in what have been hitherto considered the higher or "fine" arts of sculpture and painting. . . . A picture that is worth anything is not a piece of decoration, but a separate poem in itself; and it is better to have such works even in the company with bad furniture, than to have a room filled with decorative furniture and knick-knacks, but bare of anything that can appeal to our highest sympathies and aspirations as intellectual beings.' However most writers on interior decoration in the 1880s had no such misgivings and no matter what styles they recommended, be it for smart town house, as in the case of Colonel Edis, or suburban villa, in the case of Mrs J.E. Panton, they were all unanimous in condemning the lack of artistry in the houses of their parents. Colonel Edis wrote:[10] 'I can conceive of nothing more terrible than to be doomed to spend one's life in a house furnished after the fashion of twenty years ago. Dull monotonous walls, on which garish flock papers, of the vulgarest possible design, stare one blankly in the face with patches here and there of accumulated dirt and dust, or the even worse monstrosities of imitation *moirée* silk, with bunches of gilt flowers tied up with gilt ribbons, and running in symmetrical lines, all carefully aligned, like soldiers on parade. Of course, if the flock paper be red, we had red curtains hung on to a gigantic pole, like the mast of a ship, blossoming out at the ends into bunches of flowers, or turned finials, like enormous hyacinth bulbs in water. Of course the curtains trailed some feet on the floor, and, when not taken possession of by the pet dog or cat, became the receptacle for dust and dirt, or the hiding place of the remains of some pet's dinner. . . . An enormous glass over the miserably ugly mantelpiece, in a still more enormous gold frame, with bits of cast plaster ornament, also gilt, stuck on like bats and rats on a barn door, and like them, showing signs of decay and decomposition.'

Colonel Edis, like so many middle-class late Victorians, had an obsession with dust as a potential harbourer of germs. This is understandable at a time when tuberculosis, typhoid, cholera and many other infectious diseases were very real threats to human lives. What is less understandable is that the decorative schemes he recommended were far more cluttered than the mid-nineteenth-century interiors he so thoroughly condemns. He did, however, pioneer the use of fitted bedroom furniture in his book *Healthy Furniture and Decoration* of 1884.

Mrs Panton also shows the same concern with hygiene and the ability of the mid-nineteenth-century interior to harbour dust and dirt:[11] 'Do you recollect, I wonder, the orthodox dining rooms of twenty-five years ago? – The heavy, thick curtains of red or green cloth or moreen damask; the tremendous mahogany sideboard, generally with a cellarette underneath it, which, I recollect, made an admirable tomb in which to bury one's dolls or obnoxious books, generally triumphantly taken from the school room . . . the carpet that seemed immovable, and that was too heavy to be shaken more than once a year; and the wooly-bear hearth rug that always smelt of dust, and that was a receptacle for all sorts of cinders, toy-bricks, leaden soldiers, and bones dragged in and buried there by a delinquent dog or cat? Why, the mere shaking of that rug once a week resulted in the discovery of all sorts of treasures that had been lost, and the dust that came out was enough to choke the neighbourhood, and doubtless would have done so had the other inhabitants not all been engaged with their own.'

Unlike Colonel Edis, however, she does at least recommend such hygienic features as tiled floors, and paint surfaces which could be cleaned, but it was not until the early years of the twentieth century that rooms became noticeably lighter and simpler in appearance. Although hygiene played a considerable part in this process of simplification of interiors, one is forced to the conclusion that it was largely caused, as we shall see, by fashionable reaction to the dark, cluttered interiors of the 1880s and early 1890s.

And ultimately, it was fashion and snobbery that gave such impetus to design and decoration in England in the 1880s. As a writer in *The Builder* remarked in 1877:[12] 'This movement in the direction of good taste is, perhaps, hardly as general as is sometimes supposed . . . it has hardly reached the mass of the trading classes at all, and perhaps there are not a few among the professedly more cultured classes who are still sublimely indifferent to the designs of their tables and chairs, their carpets and wallpapers. But even these have to swim with the stream; and this indifference to the aesthetics of house furniture and decoration can hardly be openly professed by any who have the hope of social salvation.'

As a consequence of the widespread interest in design Arthur Silver's career prospered. He stated in an interview with *The Studio* magazine in 1894:[13] 'When I found, as every successful designer must needs discover sooner or later, that one pair of hands could not execute the orders which fell to my share, I attempted to bring together a body of men and establish a studio which would be capable of supplying designs for the whole field of fabrics and other materials used in the decoration of the house.' At this period (c.1880–5) he was continuing Batley's practice of providing complete interior schemes, as well as designs for textiles and wallpapers. Two delightful economical and pretty schemes survive in the Silver Studio Collection, and they reveal Arthur's talent as an aesthetic decorator (see 49, 50) but he found working for individual customers fraught with difficulties. In a lecture on stencilling given to the Architectural Association in February 1896 he stated,[18] '... the opportunities that I have had in the past for carrying out complete schemes of decoration, though not few, were so hampered by Philistine prejudices that I turned my attention more exclusively than ever to designing, and only availed myself of the rarer opportunities which occurred for unfettered treatments.'

This is hardly surprising, for one of the most exciting aspects of the 1880s and 1890s was the way in which some manufacturers devoted themselves wholeheartedly to promoting good design. Liberty, Woollams, Jeffrey and Co., and Morton were typical of these. Men such as Metford Warner, who became managing director of Jeffrey and Co. in 1872, embarked on a policy of persuading leading architects and designers to produce wallpaper designs for his firm. Sugden and Edmondson wrote:[15] 'More than any other man, Metford Warner is responsible for the place English wallpapers have taken in the forefront of the world's production of this form of decorative art. ... At a very early stage, Metford Warner resolved to make a new departure by enlisting the services of men eminent in architecture and design. He secured the co-operation of a number of prominent men like William Burges, E.W.Godwin, C.L.Eastlake and Harrison Weir ... none of whom up to that time had seriously entertained the thought of designing for wallpaper.' An advertisement for Jeffrey and Co. actually lists the designers of their wallpapers. They included A.H.Mackmurdo, Albert Moore, E.W.Godwin, Owen Jones, Lewis F.Day, Bruce Talbert and Christopher Dresser – as well as Arthur Silver. A great friend of Arthur Silver's, and one of his best and earliest customers, was Frederic Aumonier, managing director of the wallpaper manufacturer W.Woollams. His comment also reveals the support that British designers were receiving in the late nineteenth century:[16] 'Twenty five years ago the greatest number of designs for wallpapers were purchased from foreigners, principally Frenchmen ... but now foreign designs did not amount to one per cent, and he had not purchased a foreign design for seven years.'

By the mid 1890s, the Silver Studio was sufficiently well established to be able to specialise in its particularly vigorous and flamboyant form of Art Nouveau, most of which was executed by two brilliant designers, John Illingworth Kay and Harry Napper. In the 1880s, whilst the Studio was in its formative years, Arthur Silver had to be eclectic. A quote from H.J.Jennings reveals the stylistic confusion of the late nineteenth century:[17] 'For the dining room, you may have it Italian, Renaissance, Francois Premier, Elizabethan, Jacobean, Eighteenth-century English, or modern English Renaissance. French styles may be put on one side for an English dining room; so may the Gothique Anglais. . . . For the drawing room there are available the whole range of the French styles, from Louis XIV to the Empire, also the English Chippendale to Adam periods, and, if these give not scope enough, the English Renaissance as practiced by the English School.' It meant, in fact, that whilst the Silver Studio could produce an elegant and avant-garde design for Charles Knowles (see 140) it could also produce an Empire silk for Princess May of Teck's wedding dress and a design for Queen Victoria's Jubilee Plaque (see 53). However, the influence that resulted in the Silver Studio's powerful Art Nouveau designs in the 1890s are all to be seen in the Studio's work in the 1880s. In particular the following sources can be cited: Japanese Art, Renaissance ornament, William Morris, The Century Guild, Walter Crane and Albert Moore. The very earliest studio designs that could be cited as Art Nouveau date from 1885 (see 71) and obviously derive from Japanese art. Arthur Silver had been interested in Japanese art since his apprenticeship to H.W.Batley, and its influence can be seen in designs from 1875 onwards (see 50). Subsequently he collected Japanese prints and from 1888 he subscribed to S.Bing's magazine *Artistic Japan*.

The work of William Morris must be cited as another important influence on the development of the Studio's Art Nouveau. In particular, Morris's lush designs of the mid 1870s, such as *Myrtle* and *Acanthus*, bear strong resemblance in draughtsmanship, though not in colour, to the Studio's vigorous work of the mid-1890s. Of course, Arthur Silver could have arrived at the same conclusions as Morris through the study of historic textiles at the Victoria and Albert Museum, but Morris's textiles and wallpapers were so popular in the 1880s and 1890s that Arthur must have been frequently asked to provide adaptations. This fact is further confirmed by the large number of original Morris papers and textiles in the Silver Studio Collection.

Like most good designers working in the late nineteenth century, Arthur Silver frequently used the collections of historic textiles at the Victoria and Albert Museum as a source of inspiration for his own designs. Because of the popularity of these collections, Arthur Silver, in 1889, decided to launch a series of large-scale photographs of what he considered to be the most significant of these textiles, known as the Silvern Series of photographs. This enterprise attracted a considerable amount of publicity. *The Berkshire Chronicle* of 24 August 1889 stated, '. . . a valuable work . . . has been suggested by Mr Arthur Silver, son of Mr James Silver of this town. . . . A new attempt to widen the usefulness of the splendid designs in South Kensington and other national collections has been conceived and carried out by Mr Arthur Silver, himself a well-known art designer. By special permission of the ruling powers Mr Silver has selected the most suitable objects for reproduction in modern commerce. From these he has produced, by the aid of photography, full size working designs, made to the exact size commercially required by the exigencies of looms, blocks and other mechanical restrictions. These practical designs are to be sold to manufacturers, who can then reproduce the original work as accurately as if they had the actual samples before them. This new departure is one likely to influence the applied arts, for translation by a workman from a sketch, however clever, of an old fabric or other surface decoration, is almost sure to produce unintentional variations. By employing the unerring truth of the concern, the very threads of the warp and woof, or the impact of the embossing block, can be clearly seen. This enterprise, in no way officially connected with South Kensington, has been the result of years of preparatory work, and the scheme just ready for presentation to the public is likely to raise curiosity both at home and abroad, as the various state departments on the continent analagous to our South Kensington are likely to make large use of it to augment their stock of patterns from our own well-stocked museum, wherein lie hidden countless treasures practically inaccessible to those more immediately concerned manufacturers whose works are at a distance from them.'

It is significant that the Silvern Series of photographs sold steadily throughout the 1890s, in particular to the more progressive firms such as Templeton's (who also used Voysey's carpet designs), Liberty's, Simpson and Godlee and so on. Even more significant are the photographs themselves (see 90–93). For here we can see much of the original source material for designs of the late 1880s and 1890s. They fall into two distinct categories – the small formalised designs of such textiles as Near Eastern silks, of the type that had a considerable influence on Morris's work in the late 1870s and 1880s – and (by far the greatest number) large, swirling patterns of acanthus scrolls and other classical motifs from sixteenth-, seventeenth- and eighteenth-century European textiles and hangings, including Italian brocades, English embroidery and Spanish leather. Arthur Silver did not necessarily intend that these photographs shoud be copied exactly, but hoped that manufacturers would ask him to adapt them to suit contemporary taste.

As mentioned earlier, the most important designs to emerge from the Silver Studio in the nineteenth century were executed in the mid to late 1890s and they were to exercise a considerable influence not only in England but on the Continent. The Silver Studio was, in fact, one of the major British sources of Art Nouveau, and produced several thousand designs for textiles, wallpapers and metalwork in this style. The best of these were the work of John Illingworth Kay and Harry Napper. John Illingworth Kay arrived at the Silver Studio c.1892–3 and immediately produced a series of designs for furnishing textiles and wallpapers in rich clear colours on pale grounds which were stylized adaptations of Oriental landscapes with a strong vertical emphasis (see 148). Harry Napper probably arrived at the Studio slightly later, c.1894–5. His designs were even more stylized than Illingworth Kay's, and were characterised by flattened, oval flower forms, swirling upward growths and very sharply delineated outlines (see 170). Both designers suffered in some respects by working under the name of the Silver Studio, which in turn was rarely credited by the manufacturer. Nevertheless, works by both men were frequently illustrated in foreign periodicals and in particular in *Der Moderne Stil.* Such was the demand for these designs that the entire Silver Studio was given over to the production of Art Nouveau designs from 1895 to the early 1900s.

Following the success of the Silvern Series of photographs, Arthur Silver embarked on an ambitious project to popularise the recently-revived art of stencilling, primarily for wall-decoration, but also for such textiles as curtains and cushion covers. He was given considerable help and encouragement in this from his old friend Gleeson White, then editor of *The Studio* magazine. Gleeson White had already interviewed Arthur in 1894 for an article entitled 'A Studio of Design'.[18] For a second consecutive year, Arthur Silver was to be the subject of a lengthy article in *The Studio* called 'Stencilled Fabrics for Decorative Wall Hangings'.[19] These stencils won the immediate approval of protagonists of the Arts and Crafts movement by the honesty with which Arthur Silver employed the stencil plates. Rather than camouflage the joints (ties) of the stencil plates, he incorporated them into the design. Gleeson White wrote:[20] 'One feature, however, distinguishes Mr Silver's designs from some other English examples, and from most of the multi-coloured Japanese stencilled patterns. In these, . . . the necessary ties of the stencil plate have been utilised to supply the "drawing" of the designs – so far from being ignored, they are emphasised . . . so that none shall mistake the fact that the result has been secured by stencilling and by no other process.'

This stencilling venture was carried out in conjunction with Rottmann and Co. Alexander Rottmann was managing director of a firm that imported and manufactured Japanese leather and grass papers, and which had offices in Garlick Hill, in the City. Critics were delighted by this happy partnership between manufacturer and designer, and the exhibition of Rottmann-Silver Stencil decorations, launched in June 1895, received a very wide and favourable press coverage. Gleeson White wrote the introduction to the catalogue, and particularly praised Arthur Silver's use of colour:[21] 'In the early Victorian days but very few combinations of colour, most of them hopelessly bad, were deemed "cumeelfo". In the times of the aboriginal aesthetics, admixtures of citrous and peacock blues, yellowish greens and greenish-yellows, were alone held to show good taste. Their harmonies in cold gravy, and symphonies in ditch-water and duckweed were ridiculed, but copied blindly. People learned that almost any secondary or tertiary shades might be mixed without offence, and that at Liberty's one might indulge to the utmost without licence. Later on, terra-cottas, rich yellows, salmons and flame colours were added to the limited palette. From this period the striped magenta rep, and the arsenical green Brussels with bunches of lilies-of-the-valley, the scarlet table covers with black designs, and other domestic atrocities were finally discarded. Now, we begin to see that low-toned colours, even with the later additions, were mainly a compromise, which, good as it was, has already been exhausted: but, before attempting bolder harmonies, we recognise that all positive colours are to be viewed with suspicion, save when employed with great knowledge, and that "broken colour", long the joy of the artist, is at last beginning to be appreciated by people of average taste. This truth, brought home to us by a study of the glaze of Japanese pottery, and the apparent accident of fruit in Japanese fabrics, is accepted as the governing principle of these stencils. For herein the flat surfaces of monotonous pigment, hitherto the ideal of commerce, . . . are not merely avoided, but the exact opposite is deliberately sought.'

Arthur Silver had long been interested in the use of colour and had frequently and publicly criticised English use of colour, particularly when compared with the French. These stencils, with their sensitive use of colour, show a deliberate attempt to educate the British public to a more interesting and original use of colour combinations (see 156), and they must have seemed particularly fresh and vigorous at a time when heavily patterned, sombre-coloured wallpapers were in vogue.

As a result of this venture, Arthur Silver was asked to lecture before the Architectural Association on *The Modern Stencil and its Application to Interior Decoration.* It must have been particularly gratifying to him that his lecture was printed in full in both *The Building News* and *The Architect* in February 1896.

Arthur Silver died, at the peak of his career, on 28 October 1896, at the age of 43. His death was caused by heart failure, resulting from bronchitis and over-work. He had achieved a considerable amount in the sixteen years since he opened the Silver Studio. He had bought an attractive Queen Anne Revival house, No.84 Brook Green in 1884, added a Studio to it in 1886, and in 1893 had bought No.3 Haarlem Road, directly behind 84 Brook Green, also to use as a Studio. In order to do this he had been forced to borrow money from his father, friends and from a building society. With a family to provide for as well, he had, of necessity, to work extremely hard. However, there is little doubt that he was regarded as one of the great designers of the late nineteenth century – his name was frequently linked with Walter Crane, William Morris, Lewis F.Day, and Christopher Dresser in contemporary newspaper articles – and the amount of work produced by the Studio increased rapidly in the years 1890–6. As well as his photographic and stencilling projects, he had shown work at a number of exhibitions, including every Arts and Crafts Society Exhibition from 1889 to 1896, the Paris *Exposition Universelle Internationale* of 1889, and the World's Columbian Exposition at Chicago in 1893, where Voysey's work was also shown. In 1894 he contributed three chapters to Gleeson White's book *Practical Design*, on designing for woven and printed textiles and floorcloths. This work shows Arthur Silver's immense practical knowledge. In the same year he was the subject of a long article in *The Studio* magazine, and again in 1895.

But above all, his career was distinguished by an enormous and varied output of designs, nearly all of them good and some of them exceptionally so. Not only did he provide designs for a wide range of British manufacturers, some of whom such as Liberty, Warner and Sanderson, are still flourishing today but he was able, in the early 1890s, to build up a trade with French and American manufacturers. His European reputation as an avant-garde English designer was continued by Harry Napper, who took over the management of the Silver Studio in December 1896. For the next five years, almost the entire output of the Silver Studio was in various forms of Art Nouveau.

In November 1896, Harry Napper signed an agreement with Arthur Silver's widow (Isabel) to take over the complete design control of the Silver Studio, and of the staff (with the exception of Rex Silver). For this, he was offered a wage of £4.10.0d a week, plus a third share of the total net profits. In 1898, this amounted to £120, so for that year he received a salary of about £360. However, it is clear from surviving correspondence that Napper was reluctant to continue running the Studio, possibly because he was aware that Rex would take over the management as soon as he attained his majority in 1900. Also, he might well have thought that a greater income could be achieved by practising as a free-lance designer. At all events, it was after considerable persuasion on the part of Mrs Silver that he agreed to renew his contract for the year 1897–8, and in October 1898 he finally resigned as manager of the Studio. However, he maintained good relations with the Silver family and the Studio until his death in 1930. The Silvers bought his watercolour paintings (see 12, 13) and Rex Silver acted as agent for the sale of some of his designs.[22] After leaving the Studio, Napper continued to work for some of the Studio's customers, including Liberty and Alexander Rottmann. And his versatility as a designer is well illustrated in a series of interiors which he designed for the firm of Norman and Stacey Ltd, in 1902, for improved Officers' Quarters. According to the catalogue,[23] Napper was responsible for all the furniture and some of the wallpapers, light fittings, chimney pieces and metalwork. The furniture he designed was both simple and elegant, with obvious derivations from the work of Mackmurdo and Voysey. This ability to design metalwork suggests that he may have been involved in the early stages of the Silver Studio's contribution to Liberty's Cymric Silver. A surviving Silver Studio day book shows that Liberty paid the Studio for the first series of designs for Cymric Silver in October 1898, while Harry Napper was still manager. The objects listed include trays, powder bowls, pen boxes and clasps. A second invoice, again for small objects, was paid by Liberty in November 1898.[24] It is certain that some, if not all, of the earliest Silver Studio designs for Liberty Silver are by Archibald Knox (see 197 etc.) and it is possible that Napper, with his wide acquaintance amongst artists and designers, had introduced Knox to the Silver Studio and to Liberty. The Silver Studio always concentrated on designing for wallpapers and textiles, and whilst small essays into other fields were occasionally made, such as designing for book jackets and trade cards, it is unlikely that any member of the existing Studio staff would have been competent to deal with such a specialised commission. Also, because this order from Liberty was not of any great size, it is unlikely that Knox actually worked full-time at the Studio, but instead worked from home. (He was also teaching at Kingston School of Art at this time.) The Silver Studio continued to provide metalwork designs for Liberty until 1910, but after 1904 the majority seem to have been executed by Harry Silver, Rex's brother (see 229 etc.).

The Studio was managed by J. R. Houghton from 1898 to 1901, after which date Rex directed the Studio in partnership with his brother, Harry. Rex dealt with the administration of the Studio – he had been prepared for this by his father in the early 1890s[25] while Harry contributed actively as a very talented designer. Houghton left to found his own design studio at Dunmow, in Essex, and John Illingworth Kay left to run the stencilling department of Essex Wallpapers. Both Harry Napper and J. R. Houghton had continued Arthur Silver's tradition of producing avant-garde work. In fact, barely any designs were produced in historic styles over the years 1896–1900. Instead there was a constant stream of Art Nouveau designs in rich, clear colours.

A particularly important development during this period was the export of designs to Contintental manufacturers. This trend was to become so marked that by the early 1900s two-thirds of the Silver Studio's total production of designs was sold to French and Belgian textile manufacturers; and as well as the direct sale of designs abroad, a large number of Silver Studio designed textiles and wallpapers which had been produced by English manufacturers were on sale in European and American shops. Most of the major French textile manufacturers would send representatives to the Silver Studio in the autumn, probably directed there by the Studio's English customers such as Simpson and Godlee and Liberty. These included Bergert Dupont et Cie, Dumas, Florquin, Gros Roman, Zuber, Vanoutryve, Parison and Leborgne. In 1898 a total of 62 designs were sold to French textile manufacturers. In 1906, 64 designs were sold to Leborgne alone. One or two American firms began to buy designs from the Silver Studio in the early 1900s including Macy and Marshall Field, but it was not until the First World War that the American market became very important for the Studio.

The designs that both English and European manufacturers bought in the early 1900s were very different from the lush and organic productions of the mid 1890s. These designs were considerably lighter, and with marked formal qualities. They undoubtedly derive from Voysey's pattern designs of the late 1890s (a debt which Rex Silver was fully aware of, for when he wrote to Voysey he invariably addressed him as 'Dear Master'). The ordered quality of these designs is most marked in Silver Studio designs for wallpaper (see 283(b)) and it was this type of design that had so much influence on the Continent in the first quarter of this century. The tight little bunches of stylised flowers and check borders which we associate with French decorative art of the early 1920s had their origins in English pattern designs of the turn of the century.

However, whereas on the Continent English Art Nouveau was used as a basis for developing new directions in pattern design, in England it was seen merely as another style – like Louis XVI or Queen Anne, and by 1910 it was thoroughly out of date, suitable only for cheap wallpapers. A new middle-class decorating style had arisen which evoked the charms of pre-Industrial Revolution country houses, and which was characterised by light, plain walls and the use of antique furniture. Leaders of taste since the mid-nineteenth century had been calling for simple rooms containing well-designed and constructed objects and furniture and using the traditional small English country house as an example of the decorating tradition to which we should return. Amongst the most vociferous and widely publicised was, of course, William Morris, who wrote in 1880: '... this stupidity goes through all classes of society: the silk curtains in my Lord's drawing room are no more to him than the powder in his footman's hair: the kitchen in a country house is most commonly a pleasant and homelike place. ... Simplicity of life, begetting simplicity of taste, that is a love for sweet and lofty things, is of all matters most necessary for the birth of the new and better art we crave for; simplicity everywhere, in the palace as well as the cottage.' By the early 1890s, a number of architects and designers were advocating a simpler approach to decoration, and, like William Morris, they frequently referred to unspoilt small country-house interiors as an infinitely more satisfactory alternative to over-elaborate and dark middle-class interiors, and also as a basis for working-class decorating. Typical of these was William Lethaby, who wrote a number of articles in the 1890s aimed specifically at educating the taste of the working class, which as a consequence were couched in terms both simple and patronising. In 'Simple Furniture', an essay which appeared in *Plain Handicrafts* published in 1892,[26] the furniture he suggests is envisaged in a plain, whitewashed setting, based on a Yorkshire farmhouse interior. This article is particularly useful as he is specific about materials, construction and colours. 'If, being able to do good work, you are going to make your room pleasant to live in, whitewash the walls and ceiling; put a little ochre in the wash, but do not on any account use blue for the walls, it is extremely disagreeable. Paint the woodwork a light "buff" or stone colour; some parts, like the skirting, may be black if you like, or the whole can be green, nearly any tint of which will do if you do not call it "Peacock" and think that it is artistic.' Having described suitable plain furniture for the room he finishes by saying: 'Should you make all these, with a book case which you must yourself design – I think you might buy a nice clock – then with some flowers in the window, a cat, and good plain things to eat, I am sure you ought to be happy.' Edward Prior, the architect, also stressed the need for a return to a simpler way of life, with sound craftsmanship, honest values and wholesome food:[27] '... Our houses have been built for the most part with nothing in view but their saleable quality ... moreover, see how the utility of workmanship has suffered by the custom of rating its value by the price paid for it. Competition, having crushed the special excellence, has turned its weapon on its own productions, and establishing everywhere the cheap substitute in place of the genuine article. We have to take not only what does not suit us, but what is not the real thing at all – fatty compounds for butter, glucose for sugar, chemicals for beer, and just as certainly the sham house for the real building, its style a counterfeit, its construction a saleable make-believe, its carved wood a pressing from machinery, its panelling lineoleum, its plaster some pulp or other, its metalwork a composition, its painted glass only paper – everything charmingly commercial and everything charmingly cheap. We have lots of beer; we have lots of ornament in our houses; arsenic in the one, and sheer humbug in the other. Let the twentieth century contrive at least to get its goods wholesome and its ornaments hand-made.'

Unfortunately, most people could not afford hand-made ornament unless it was in the form of inherited antique furniture, or old ornaments and homely country-made eighteenth-century furniture from small antique shops. The products of the Arts and Crafts movement were much too expensive for all but the rich. Thus the protagonists of the Arts and Crafts movement simply encouraged the craze for collecting antiques and restoring country cottages, to the detriment of both modern architecture and design. *Country Life*, and books on modern architecture from 1900 onwards, were filled with photographs of charming interiors, all more or less identical, with bare, light walls, antique furniture, oriental rugs and comfortable sofas covered in chintz of chinoiserie design. Astute critics quickly realised what was happening, but such was the sentiment for a pre-Industrial-Revolution England, that any attempts to emulate developments on the Continent met with considerable criticism. One critic wrote in the *Studio Year Book* of 1907:[28] 'In the early days of the Arts and Crafts movement, the eyes of all Europe were turned towards England as the strenuous leader of a great artistic revival. Today the Continental nations look no more to her for light and guidance, but, having borrowed once and for all what pleased their fancy to adopt, they are even now proceeding to develop and elaborate it in their several ways, quite independently. Some of them, indeed, disregarding the elementary laws of construction and the claims of their material, have run to the wildest of extravagances. Others, on the contrary, seizing upon the simple motif of plain straight lines and quadratic forms in construction, have raised up a national ideal of their own, which bids fair to surpass the most brilliant essays in that direction ever achieved in Great Britain itself.'

Just as Arthur Silver had done, Rex saw the necessity of being able to produce designs in a wide variety of styles. As the vogue for Art Nouveau designs declined in the early 1900s, he concentrated increasingly on the production of designs in period styles. Like his father, he listened carefully to the requests of his clients, suggesting potential sources of designs and possible colour schemes. He would in turn issue very specific information to his staff of designers, giving them cuttings of similar material and again suggesting potential sources for the design. Rex does not seem to have actually designed very much himself, but Harry Silver, his brother and partner (until 1916), was very actively involved in designing. Harry was responsible for all the later designs for Liberty's Cymric Silver and Tudoric Pewter from the Silver Studio, and whilst some of these have Celtic ornamental detail which would suggest the influence of Archibald Knox, others are in an elegant neo-Adam style (see 244). The Silver Studio's prospective entry for *The Studio Year Book Directory of Designers* of 1909 was as follows: 'Messrs R. and H. Silver are young designers who work together at their Studios at No.3 Haarlem Road, Brook Green, W, with two or three young assistants to aid them in carrying out their ideas. They lay themselves out to supply designs in the different styles both ancient and modern and owing to their knowledge of the different branches of weaving and printing etc., all their designs for such purposes as Wallpapers, Cretonnes, Tapestries, etc., are thoroughly practical. They are also able to design and carry out schemes for interior decoration and are able to use for this purpose certain new stencilling processes which enable them to obtain very individual and complete effects for walls and all kinds of

I
Design for a wallpaper, c.1890 (104b)

II
Design for a decoration of a door and wall, c.1885 (49)

III a and b
Designs for a rug, 1934 (445)

III c
Design for a printed textile, 1903 (293)

III d
Design for a rug, 1934 (445)

IV a
Woven silk and cotton cloth, c.1900 (284)

IV b
Woven silk and cotton doublecloth, 1898 (250)

IV c
Design for a printed textile, 1892 (116)

hangings – combining the two to make complete decorations to rooms etc.'

The stencilling process referred to met with only limited success. Rex had purchased for £15 a recipe for light- and water-fast stencil colours from a firm of block printers, Berners Seager and Clark, which enabled the Studio staff not only to stencil wallcoverings but bedspreads, curtains, cushion covers and so forth. Customers were found either through personal recommendation or through certain of the Studio's customers, such as Franklin and Auerbach and Simpson and Godlee. Although this process could produce charming results it was not suitable for any large-scale production. The colours had a horrid smell which lasted for a few weeks after being applied, and were difficult to use. Simpson and Godlee wrote complaining of a consignment of stencilled bedspreads:[29] 'We regret very much that the spreads have proved so unsatisfactory that we certainly cannot encourage you to make further outlay. The goods are practically all imperfect. In many cases, there are smears of colour upon the ground, and in others, stains of various kinds. We have had several lots returned to us, and as we shall have to treat those on hand as job goods, you will see that we can hold out little hope of placing further orders. We are very disappointed with this result, and of course it must be disappointing to you, but really the goods are unsaleable in the normal way.'

As their new stencilling process was obviously not going to prove a commercial success, Rex and Harry decided to concentrate instead on the Studio's traditional role of producing designs for textiles and wallpapers.

Rex Silver became engaged to Ruby Orchard in 1911, and towards the end of that year bought No.1 Haarlem Road to use both as a Studio and as a future house for himself and his bride. 84 Brook Green was let, and No.3 Haarlem Road, the old Studio premises, was sold shortly after this date. At the same time, Rex and Harry took on more staff. In 1908 there had been only two full-time assistants – Herbert Crofts and Lewis Jones. By 1912 there were seven – viz. Herbert Crofts, Lewis Jones, R.Hughes, E.Parker, Edwin Jeffrey, John Van Teffelen and Winifred Mold. Winifred Mold is still living and she described in a letter how she came to work for the Silver Studio:[30] 'As a child I was fond of drawing. When I left school, I went to a private studio run by my former drawing mistress at school, Miss F.Kendrick. She taught me the rudiments of design, starting on damask napkins and tablecloths. I liked designing, so after 1909 I joined the art department of the Paddington Technical Institute under a Mr Walker. The majority of the work I did there was for wallpapers. About 1911, Mr Walker left and I thought I would strike out on my own, but I did not know where to sell my designs. I went first to John Lines of Tottenham Court Road, but they did not need any. Then I tried Sandersons who advised me to send samples of my work to Rex Silver. That was in January 1912. He agreed to take me on as an apprentice at a wage of 2s 6d a week. I did my work at home as I was the only girl employed, and taking it when finished to the Studio.' Miss Mold was also able to describe the designers' working methods, which were probably those first practised by Arthur Silver. (The methods described by Miss Mold remained unchanged until the Silver Studio closed.) 'The method then, was to do a miniature $\frac{1}{8}$th size of the finished design and when accepted (by a manufacturer) to enlarge it on to whitey-brown paper. The next thing was to make a tracing and try out colour schemes, finally transferring the design to stretched cartridge paper and painting it. Rex Silver used to give me a rough idea of the type of design he wanted, the size of the subject, period and the number of colours to use. Then he left it to me. I used to bring him my designs for him to criticise, discuss and suggest alterations.'

The designs produced by the Silver Studio over the period 1912–20 were mostly in a variety of period styles, ranging from chinoiserie chintz designs, with flowering branches, tropical birds and large flowers, such as peonies and cabbage roses, to elegant neo-Adam designs with vases and acanthus scrolls. The source for these designs was often the Victoria and Albert Museum, and Winifred Mold recalls Rex Silver encouraging his staff to go there.

Of all the designers working at the Silver Studio between 1905 and the First World War, Harry Silver seems to have been the most versatile and talented. As well as producing excellent period designs of superb draughtsmanship, he was one of the first British designers to show work influenced by the costumes and sets of the Russian ballet. Using brilliant colours, he produced a number of designs inspired by Russian folk art between 1912 and 1916 and even a design of flat, stylised flowers in a basket which was to become a characteristic motif of French decorative art in the 1920s. (He had probably seen similar work by André Groualt in the *Studio Year Book* of 1914.) The Silvers were enthusiastic concert-goers and may well have seen a performance of the Russian Ballet. At this time, too, they were still selling designs to French manufacturers and would have been encouraged to use the brilliant colours that were rapidly becoming fashionable in France in the years immediately preceding the First World War. Even in England there were one or two firms – notably Heals and Foxtons – who were trying to persuade the English middle classes to buy simple furniture and elegant textiles of abstract design but such efforts were met with considerable resistance. Horace Warner wrote in *The Studio Year Book* for 1915:[31] 'Recently we have seen a demand, which originated on the Continent, for violent colours and strange designs. But this has not found any response amongst the designers of English wallpapers, nor is it reflected in the taste of art lovers for the decoration of their walls. After all, nothing can replace those patterns which are sound in construction and drawing, harmonious in colouring, and which have been designed by British artists for British homes. Moreover they have stood the test of years amidst the passing of many fashions.' In England at least, it once more became rather affected to profess too great an interest in decoration, and particularly modern decoration. This was partly due to the frightfulness of some writers on interior decoration. Typical of these was Hall Thorpe who wrote an article for *The Studio* entitled 'On Colour in the Cottage'[32]. It starts like a house-agent's advertisement for Metro-Land. 'There is a country walk I love to take that leads by narrow footpaths across fields of corn and clover and on through beech woods, where my eyes are rested in soft colours and subdued light, until out again I come to find a lovely view of open country and just at hand a most ideal English village tucked away among old trees and gardens, and hedged about with farmlands. I am filled afresh with joy and wonder to think how it all came to be so exactly right – the old ivied church, the manor house, the village green, the horse-pond, and box hedges, and the dearest little inn are all there, just in their right places. . . . But of all its attractions, I was most in love with the labourers' cottages with their little gardens of old world flowers.' He then proceeds to be very rude about the labourers' taste in decoration: 'The quaint haphazard shapes of their cottages always awakened in me a longing to know what the rooms inside were like – they promised so many possibilities – and I could well imagine how wonderful the landscape would look framed in their long narrow windows. Set in such lovely country and looking so beautiful without, I felt they must be equally beautiful and interesting within; and I still remember the shock and disappointment I received when I first entered them and found the walls covered with ugly patterned papers of unpleasant colours and thickly hung with Christmas supplements and enlarged photographs of the family. Although the rooms were a good shape, they were spoilt by being crowded up by many useless oddments, and the lovely view I had hoped to see through the windows was only visible through the mesh of Nottingham Lace curtains.' He describes the decorative efforts of two women who had purchased a similar cottage in terms of such artful coyness that it is little wonder that the owners of 'artistic' cottages in the 1920s were guyed by so many writers. 'They had learned by experience that a bright effect in a room is not obtained by piling in a lot of colour, but in a wise proportion and juxtaposition of tones, the combination of a few simple colours being much safer and more successful than the use of many. Definite rules were observed in the choice of these articles, and in selecting them they were considered more as expressions of thought than as material things. Thus a bowl of beautiful colour and fine shape, with a narrow well-designed bacchanalian frieze of fauns and satyrs, was rejected because of the evil influence of the god of wine. A gaily patterned fabric that was just the thing for a certain scheme, was regretfully laid aside when it was found that a stag was being chased through its foliage.'

By the outbreak of the First World War, Rex and Harry had a staff of eleven designers and four apprentices. Business was extremely good, partly because of the demand in the United States for English printed furnishing textiles. (Elsie de Woolfe, the American interior decorator, had started a craze for old-fashioned English chintz by using it in her scheme for the Colony Club in New York in 1906 and in subsequent important commissions.) Business continued to be excellent for the duration of the war, as the United States were dependent on Britain for textiles, with supplies no longer available from France and Germany. Firms like Wardles, Simpson and Godlee, Denby and Franklin had a flourishing export trade with the States and this provided the Silver Studio with a great deal of work. The designs that were most in demand were for exquisitely drawn Chinoiserie chintzes in rich colours and the firms involved were most anxious that the Silver Studio be kept going to provide these. Unfortunately, five of the Studio designers, including Harry Silver, were conscripted. Despite desperate efforts on the part of Rex Silver and the above-mentioned firms, Rex himself was conscripted in 1917 and the Studio closed for over a year. Rex spent six miserable months in the Labour corps, and then a year in the Ministry of National Service under Sir Auckland Geddes.

Rex had tragically lost his wife in 1917 after only two years of marriage – she had died of a heart attack. An additional blow was that his brother Harry decided not to return to the Studio after the Armistice had been declared. It seems that Harry felt that the Studio would not support the two of them and instead he opened a garage and motor repair works in North London. Harry continued to maintain a close interest in the Studio, and regularly met Rex on Thursday afternoons to discuss business matters. In 1918 Rex acquired an excellent secretary, Miss Florence Cook, who stayed with the Studio until 1940 and who maintained accurate records of the Studio's operations for the whole of this period.

By 1920, the Studio was virtually back to its pre-war strength, with most of the former design staff having returned. Two excellent new designers joined the Studio – Madeleine Lawrence, who like Winifred Mold worked from home, and Frank Price, who stayed with the Studio until 1963, apart from a short period at Sandersons. Frank Price was one of the best designers to have worked in the Studio after Archibald Knox, and was responsible for some superb work in the 1930s and after the Second World War (see 514).

The immediate post-war years were characterised by a striking division of taste in interior decoration. The upper and middle classes continued to be very much in favour of period design – the sentiment for Old England having been given renewed vigour by the war. Lower down the social scale there was a demand for cheap textiles and wallpapers of exotic design and in brilliant colours. The decorating tastes of the middle classes were catered for by *House and Garden*, which first appeared in November 1920. For those of modest income it recommended the acquisition and conversion of a country cottage and particularly recommended Rye and Winchelsea as fruitful hunting grounds for quaint cottages. E.F. Benson, who brilliantly describes the inhabitants of Rye in the 1920s and 1930s in his *Mapp and Lucia* novels, illustrated with great accuracy the upper-middle-class interest in Neo-Tudor and Georgian decorating that was fashionable between the wars. Describing the cottage of Mrs Emmeline Lucas at Riseholme (a thinly disguised Broadway), he wrote:[33] 'So when there were sufficient thousands of pounds in firm securities, she had easily persuaded him to buy three . . . cottages that stood together in a low two-storied block, and had, by judicious removal of partition walls, transmuted them into a most comfortable dwelling, subsequently adding on a new wing running out at right-angles at the back, which was, if anything , a shade more blatantly Elizabethan than the stem to which it was grafted, for here was situated the famous smoking parlour, with rushes on the floor, a dresser ranged with pewter tankards, and leaded lattice-windows of glass so antique that it was practically impossible to see out of them. It had a huge open fire-place framed in oak beams, with a seat on each side of the iron-backed hearth within the chimney, and an iron spit hung over the middle of the fire. Here, though in the rest of the house she had, for the sake of convenience, allowed the installation of electric light, there was no such concession made, and the sconces on the walls held dim iron lamps, so that only those of the most acute vision were able to see to read. Even to them reading was difficult, for the bookstand on the table contained nothing but a few crabbed black-letter volumes dating from not later than the early seventeenth century, and you had to be in a fanatically Elizabethan frame of mind to be at ease there. But Mrs Lucas often spent rare leisure moments there, playing on the virginal that stood in the window, or kippering herself in the smoke of the wood-fire as with streaming eyes she deciphered an Elsevir Horace, rather late for inclusion under the rule, but an undoubted bargain.'

Although a small section of British Society was interested in developments that were taking place in France, and could see the virtues of abstract pattern designing, it was not until the late 1920s that Cubism made any impact on British decorative art. This was despite the efforts of Roger Fry and the fact that the work of Robert and Sonia Delaunay would have been made known to British ballet-lovers at least, in the 1919 production of *Cléopâtre* at the Coliseum. W. Turnbull of Turnbull and Stockdale (one of the Silver Studio's best customers) wrote in 1923:[34] 'Prejudice against certain styles has always hindered the [Art] schools from being really useful to the trade. I was brought up under the late Lewis F. Day, who was for many years our art director, and so my predilection runs in direction of the purely conventional. It is obvious, though, that the majority of people who use cretonnes, etc., prefer a frankly naturalistic style of design. Now the schools have never given this style a chance. It is all very well to damn the style as inherently bad – it is only bad if badly done. After all, "convention" enters into even the most "naturalistic" type. The Early Victorian period was responsible, doubtless, for much that was bad, but who will deny the inherent rightness of the chintzes produced about 1840? Now why should the schools block the way of a student whose method of self-expression obviously runs to the "naturalistic"? How much wiser would it be to see that he is taught to appreciate light and shade as applied to flower studies. I bought a design once from one of our most successful designers, which contained several quite conventional roses, and he told me that he made at least fifty studies of roses from nature for the purpose of that particular design. Needless to say he had got his highlights exactly where they ought to be! And yet the schools seem to look down on the producer who wants good floral designs. And so our students cannot find work, and our printers spend thousands of pounds in Paris.'

The success of English period design in the States continued through the 1920s, and Rex Silver was able to count Macey's and Marshall Field amongst his best customers. He even found it worthwhile to employ a representative in the United States – J. R. Doughty – in the mid 1920s to sell Silver Studio designs to American manufacturers. This arrangement, however, was discontinued in 1927 when Rex discovered that Doughty had been keeping money from sales to customers.

In 1923, Rex Silver was interviewed by the *Christian Science Monitor*, and in this article he made it perfectly clear that his own preference was very much for well-drawn and sensitively coloured designs based on historical styles:[35] 'The very wide scope of the designs found in modern furnishing fabrics was recently pointed out by Reginald Silver in his Studio of Design in London. Mr Silver is carrying on the work started by his father who was a contemporary and friend of William Morris.

'"Design is on the upward trend", he said. "We have become less 'groovy', and though we are using tradition, it is to a much freer way so that we are making things suited to the present broader outlook. The producers look to the designers to help them to lead fashion in the right direction artistically, in the effort to improve the public taste generally. The designers also have to watch the modern methods of production and their endeavor is to help to give freshness to the old ideas. We specialize in designs for printed linens and cottons, based on old silks and embroideries," continued Mr Silver, "because we find that people are looking for fabrics suited to rooms decorated in different periods. If they are sufficiently keen, they consult their architects in order to be sure of getting something in keeping, so we have to work with the architects. In fact, nowadays, to be a designer, you have to be *au fait* with all the traditional styles. The Victoria and Albert Museum is a great inspiration, but it is no use just copying old pieces, because everybody is doing that. If you want to make a design of a particular period, you have to get imbued with the spirit of that period and imagine that you are a designer in those days and are carrying on their tradition. We also want to keep up our originality, and that is what I think we are doing. English designs are holding their own very well now, and English styles and work are wanted all over the world." The first ideas for the designs for fabrics are made in charcoal and coloured chalks or pastels on large sheets of rough paper, measuring about five feet square and a number of them were hung one over the other on the study wall. There was a delightful Queen Anne chintz design with delicate little bouquets of flowers and humming birds fluttering around them, which called up a picture of a room with high-backed chairs and fragrant with the scent of blossoms wafted in through open windows from an old-world garden. "Birds are being so much used", said Mr Silver, "that people say 'We won't have any more.' but they always have them all the same! They are very helpful in a design. In a second colored cartoon for an old English chintz, delicious pink roses, mauve and pink tulips, and Canterbury bells were carelessly and gracefully grouped on an ivory background. Another cartoon showed a procession of Chinese dragon boats, passing down through a series of lakes, broken by clumps of trees, forming an unusual and interesting subject.

'"That," said Mr Silver, "was based on an old Chinese Painting at the Victoria and Albert Museum. It was just a tiny picture, and a practical interpretation of it had to be made to suit modern methods of production."'

'"A surprisingly unusual design, of which the blocks are just being cut preparatory to putting it on the market in the form of a printed linen, was of a combined land and seascape in soft old Morland coloring, with sailing ships of the Nelson type. This is intended to be used as a background in the shape of panels in a room or on a screen.

'"The designer also needs to keep in touch with the modern movements, some of which are very fine and some very bad." Mr Silver went on. "Futurism, for instance, is not a movement that I am very fond of, though Futurist methods suit certain purposes where you want an excuse for broken color. But it is really on the wane here and I think even in France. More drawing is wanted, more form. The Futurist type of design does not mean enough – anyone can make Futurist designs. But I think that now there will be much more chance for people who can really draw, and I feel that designers who can give vent to their imaginations in a more coherent and happier way will come into their own. There are quite good modern productions based on Chinese traditions. They come out very well in linen or good imitation of linen, and also in brocade. Chinese designs are very popular because they go with Chippendale furniture. Some of the strictly modern designs show a decided Japanese influence. I am very fascinated by Japanese art myself. Here is a design that the manufacturers cannot print fast enough. It shows a strong Japanese influence and has, as you see, a primrose ground with a foliage trail in tones of gray, little birds lit up with orange and gray and a flower with just a touch of orange in it. Most of these printed cottons are done with backgrounds in several different colors. This one is also in matrix-blue, dark blue, black and orange.

'"Color is very important nowadays, quite as important as design, and the chemists have helped us much in this. The improvement in color has been one of the cardinal changes in furnishing fabrics during the last 20 years. The possibilities formerly were much more limited because you could not get fast colors with subtle differences in them that you could rely on as you can now, and we are trying to make people realise the beauty of these subtleties of color. The Futurists of course go in for brilliant splashes of primary colors. They say 'Let us have brilliant color for happiness'. But things can be 'happy' even if they are a little quieter and we are getting people to appreciate the secondary and tertiary colors. I want to teach them to like simplified color effects, as for instance two tones of color on a white ground. You can arrive at very restful effects in this way."

'A still further insight was gained into the very wide range covered by the designs of today, when, before leaving the study, the writer glanced through a little sheaf of color notes that had been made previous to preparing the big cartoons.

'"It would take too long", Mr Silver said, "to put them down on the large size until you know if the idea is worth developing."

'Remarkably varied both as regards color and form were these miniature designs, from a Watteau scheme with little figure panels to a modern design with a brownish floral trellis based on a Grinling Gibbons carving.'

This article is important, because it gives an insight into Rex Silver's interest in the subtle use of colour which enabled him to win the custom of Liberty's for very many of their dress and furnishing textiles in the late 1920s and 1930s. The use of brilliant colour was indeed a short-lived phase, and largely confined to cheaper wallpapers and textiles. The Silver Studio provided a number of designs for the manufacturers of cheap wallpapers and textiles in the early 1920s, but they were far from satisfactory customers. Novelty was placed at a high premium – the discovery of Tutankahmen's Tomb in 1922 prompted a spate of Eyptian designs as did the success of the film *The Sheik* which resulted in wallpaper friezes depicting romantic desert landscapes, with palm trees, pyramids and minarets. These manufacturers paid very badly, and gave scant attention to draughtsmanship. The bulk of the designs executed by the Studio for these firms were in a rather crude form of eighteenth-century chinoiserie, invariably in brilliant colours which imitated eighteenth-century lacquer work, and which were regarded as ideal accompaniments to reproduction eighteenth-century furniture.

However, even in the very early 1920s there were indications of a reaction against the use of genuine and fake antique furniture and textiles based on period designs. As early as 1920 Harrods advertised furnishing textiles with designs inspired by Scandinavian peasant art and Coles Ltd, had begun importing modern French wallpapers from about the same date.

There can be little doubt that the Paris Exhibition of Decorative Art of 1925 gave considerable impetus to the growing interest in modern design. Rex Silver attended it with a party of delegates from the Design and Industries Association, and, shortly after his return to England, purchased volumes of plates by two leading French pattern designers – Seguy and Edward Benedictus which were to provide the inspiration for a number of Silver Studio designs in the late 1920s and early 1930s.

By the late 1920s, one or two periodicals were making a concerted effort to encourage more people to buy modern designs. And indeed, the time was right for a reaction against the older generations' consistent use of antique furniture and furnishings. One of the most influential of these periodicals was undoubtedly *Ideal Home*, whose market was largely the purchasers of new semi-detached houses in the outer suburbs. *Ideal Home*, as well as promoting labour-saving equipment regularly showed work by leading European designers from 1928 onwards. At first, illustrations of furniture by Gio Ponti and room sets by Maurice Dufrene fought for space alongside Stockbroker Tudor interiors, but by 1933, the cosy chintz-filled interiors had largely been ousted by illustrations of modern rooms, featuring the work of Scandinavian, as well as French and Italian, designers. One writer for *Ideal Home*, Muriel Harris, recommended a nursery by Djo-Bourgeois in 1928:[36] 'It is true that so far the Cubist baby bears a strong resemblance to other babies. The difference is that he is being given a clean sheet upon which to inscribe his ideas.'

At the same time, there was a growing fashion for naturalistic floral printed dress and furnishing textiles, in clear colours and usually on a light ground. This seems to have been largely promoted by Liberty's, and using designs from the Silver Studio. Such was the demand for these designs, both from Liberty and other firms who were quick to imitate this style, that the Silver Studio was able to survive the collapse of the American market following the Wall Street Crash, and the Depression, more or less unscathed. Josephine Hawkes wrote in 1928:[37] 'Today you will find the cretonnes, the hand-block printed linens and the chintzes reflecting to perfection flowers of every country and clime. Because of the exquisite natural tones and shades of tones in the modern dyes, the last word in flower designing for fabrics is to depict the flowers in natural form, colour and habitat. The "naturalness" of the flower fabric enables us to have a garden of fabric flowers inside our homes, and a colour atmosphere that is a constant reminder of sun-filled days.'

Modern French pattern design gained increasing acceptance in England in the early 1930s, though the strong colours of French designs were replaced by softer hues, particularly shades of brown. The early 1930s also saw one or two enterprising firms such as Warner, Donald Brothers and Morton producing simply textured woven furnishing fabrics, which were immediately very successful. Pevsner in his report on 'The Designer in Modern Industry' in the *Architectural Review* of 1936 wrote:[38] '... the state of affairs in English woven fabrics is undeniably gratifying.' This article illustrated a woven textile designed by the Silver Studio for Warner. Donald Brothers also bought many similar loose check designs for their *Old Glamis* range of furnishing textiles. However, in the early 1930s at least, these manufacturers were very much the exception. The Depression had made most firms adopt a conservative attitude to design, and they bought only those designs which they knew would be saleable. Even Simpson and Godlee, the Studio's most adventurous client for printed textiles, only infrequently commissioned modern designs until the late 1930s – and the 'modern' designs they took in the early 1930s were based on French avant-garde work of the early 1920s. The American market had been badly affected by an excise duty on all foreign designs imported into the United States. And when Rex Silver returned to Paris in 1931 to try and recapture some of his former French customers by offering them naturalistic floral designs, he found that French manufacturers were equally affected by the Depression, with no more rich Americans to buy their luxury goods.

However, by 1935, there were distinct signs of improvement. The interest in Scandinavian design was beginning to grow, encouraged by the Stockholm Exhibition of 1930. From 1936 it was possible to buy bentwood furniture by Alvar Aalto at a very reasonablé price, and with easy terms, from Bowmans of Camden Town and other large department stores. (Bowmans also advertised rugs by Marion Dorn and furniture by Marcel Breuer.) *Ideal Home* magazine now very rarely illustrated anything but the most sophisticated modern interiors which featured very bare walls, and textiles of undemonstrative design, usually woven rather than printed.

But the revived interest in the Rococo and in the Regency periods, which seems to have begun in the late 1920s in America, and whose leading exponent in England in the 1930s was Syrie Maughan, provided the Silver Studio with the opportunity to produce some exquisite designs for printed textiles based on the work of Rex Whistler and Duncan Grant. Designs including flowers inspired by seventeenth-century Dutch still-life paintings combined with Rococo scrolls and cartouches were beautifully drawn and sensitively coloured by Frank Price.

By the outbreak of the Second World War the output of the Silver Studio was larger and more varied than at any other time in its history. The period designs produced included neo-Regency, neo-Rococo, simple early nineteenth-century chintzes and seventeenth-century needlework designs. There were simple textured patterns for woven textiles, and single-leaf motifs for woven and printed textiles. Geometric designs for wallpapers and textiles were still very popular, as were the naturalistic floral motifs in bright colours used for both furnishing and dress fabrics. Designs inspired by Scandinavian art were becoming increasingly popular in the late 1930s, and so were designs based on motifs from Persian tribal art.

This period of prosperity enjoyed by the Studio in the late 1930s was brought to an end by the outbreak of the Second World War. Rex was now nearly 60 and he saw little hope of keeping the Studio going. Accordingly he dismissed nearly all of his staff, including the two secretaries, Miss Cook and Miss Varney, so that by the summer of 1940 there was only Frank Price – who was too severely disabled to be conscripted – left working in the studio, and two outside designers – H.C. Bareham and Madeleine Lawrence. At the end of the war, Rex's oldest member of staff, Lewis Jones, returned to work with Frank Price at the Studio. A plan by Rex to offer Lewis Jones and Frank Price a partnership in the Studio ended with Jones's death in 1952. Once more, Frank Price was the only designer working in the Silver Studio, and remained so until 1963, when Rex Silver finally closed the Studio. Madeleine Lawrence had died in 1951, though H.C. Bareham continued to work from his house until 1963. Through the war and up until the early 1960s, the Silver Studio specialised in providing neo-eighteenth-century and Regency designs – largely for the Studio's oldest customers – R. Denby and Sons, Liberty, Sanderson, Simpson and Godlee, Turnbull and Stockdale, Warner and G.P. and J. Baker. Rex was used to dealing with these firms, who in turn could rely on the Silver Studio to provide a particularly special period design. Frank Price's talents were admirably suited to producing fashionable elegant designs for chintzes inspired by old prints or eighteenth-century architectural ornament. Although Frank Price left the Studio in 1963, Rex continued to sell designs by him until 1965. Rex died in the September of that year, and amongst the letters received by his step daughter, Miss Mary Peerless, was an especially touching one from Rex's two secretaries – Miss Florence Cook and Miss E.M. Varney. Florence Cook wrote:[39] 'Dear Miss Peerless, We very much appreciated your letting us know about Mr Silver so that we could get to the cemetery and pay our last respects to him. We worked with him for a long time and always found him very kind and considerate. He worked very hard himself and always got on very well with his employees and his business associates. He had dealings with many American firms before the war and had many friends in Manchester and in the North, as well as in and around London. He was always willing to help young people and found the time and patience to look at their efforts and give them advice. The business of Decorative Design has been carried out by the Silvers for many years at 84 Brook Green and then at Corner House Haarlem Road and the good work turned out from the Silver Studio was well known. Absolute perfection in every detail, however small the commission, was essential to him. We shall always remember him with affection and admiration.'

The Silver Studio always suffered from the custom of manufacturers not to credit the designers of their products. Aymer Vallance, writing of the death of Arthur Silver in 1896, in *The Studio* magazine, said:[40] '... by the death of this very accomplished designer, the applied arts have lost a staunch ally. To improve the level of manufactured articles is perhaps the most arduous effort that confronts a designer. His patron may be a man of taste willing to experiment and not always deterred by unprofitable ventures; but even the most artistic merchant has to face the balance-sheet and the comments of his salesman. The designer for the trade has a double duty – to art first but also to commerce. He must be competent to produce schemes which are capable of being carried out economically and do not repel buyers. Mr Silver's zeal for art was perhaps only fully realised by those who knew him intimately, but not even Mr William Morris himself was more eager to beautify the articles of daily life. And while the wares of one were out of the reach of the great middle and lower classes, much of the work of the other was expended on cheap material. Owing to the anonymity of the inventor being rigidly preserved by most manufacturers, dozens of people who bought and appreciated Mr Silver's designs never dreamed who was responsible for them.'

It is hoped that this exhibition will to some extent rectify the unjustified neglect of the Silver Studio and the designers who worked there.

1. I am grateful to Michael Curtis, Librarian at Reading Central Library for this and other biographical information on the Silver Family.
2. Robert W. Edis: *The Decoration and Furniture of Town Houses*, 1881, p.6.
3. H.W.Batley in the introduction to his book *A Series of Studies for Domestic Furniture*, 1882.
4. Alexander Millar: 'Design in Modern Carpets', 1894 published in *The Journal of the Society of Arts*, 20 April 1894, p.435. (Alexander Millar also praises Arthur Silver's designs for carpets in this article.)
5. Catalogue of the Guild of Decorators Syndicate Ltd, 1908. (In the Silver Studio Collection, Middlesex Polytechnic.)
6. Letter from W.H.Walenn to Arthur Silver, dated 17 February 1878. (In the Silver Studio Collection, Middlesex Polytechnic.)
7. Mrs J.E.Panton: *In Garrett and Kitchen*, 1919, p.18.
8. Article reprinted in *The Building News*, 1874, p.23.
9. *The Builder*, 6 October 1877, p.1002, under the title 'Is the present taste for "Art Furniture" and Bric a Brac indicative of a sound or healthy Aesthetic culture'.
10. Robert W.Edis: *The Decoration and Furniture of Town Houses*, 1881, pp.17–20.
11. Mrs J.E.Panton: *From Kitchen to Garrett*, 1889, pp.7–8.
12. *The Builder*, 6 October 1877, p.1002.
13. Arthur Silver: 'A Studio of Design' in *The Studio*, Vol. III, 1894, p.117.
14. The original typescript of the lecture is in the Silver Studio Collection. It is reprinted in full in *The Building News*, 16 February 1896, pp.305–7, *The Journal of Decorative Arts*, June 1896, pp.152–5 and *The Architect*, 28 February 1896, pp.141–4.
15. A.V.Sugden and J.L.Edmondson: *A History of English Wallpaper*, 1925, p.210.
16. *The Builder*, 6 October 1877, p.1002.
17. H.J.Jennings: *Our Homes and How to Beautify Them*, 1901, pp.73–4.
18. *The Studio*, Vol. III, p.117–22.

19. *The Studio*, Vol. v, pp.181–5.
20. *ibid.*, p.182.
21. Gleeson White: *Some Notes on Stencilling*. Catalogue introduction for Arthur Silver's exhibition of stencils held at Rottmann's in 1895.
22. Rex Silver sold designs by Harry Napper throughout the 1920s, charging commission of one-third of the selling price.
23. See Catalogue *Officers' Ideal Quarters* published by Norman and Stacey Ltd, 1902 in the Silver Studio Collection, Middlesex Polytechnic.
24. See *The Silver Studio Day Book 1892–8* in the Silver Studio Collection.
25. Arthur Silver wrote to Rex in Manchester on 6 September 1896 with information to help him on his first design-selling trip to the North-country manufacturers.
26. The article 'Simple Furniture' by W. R. Lethaby, although first published in 1892 in a small volume called *Plain Handicrafts*, Percival and Co., was reprinted as a pamphlet by the Dryad Works, Leicester for the Design and Industries Association, c.1920.
27. Edward S. Prior: 'Upon Home Building in the 20th C.', in *The Studio*, Special Summer Number, 1901, pp.9–14.
28. *The Studio Year Book*, 1907, pp.2–3.
29. From a letter by L. V. Gladwell of Simpson and Godlee, Ltd, 24 May 1910, in the Silver Studio Collection.
30. From a letter to the Keeper of the Silver Studio Collection by Winifred Mold, December 1976.
31. Horace Warner: 'Wallpaper Designers and their Work', in *The Studio Year Book*, 1915, p.170.
32. *The Studio Year Book*, 1919, pp.65–70.
33. E. F. Benson: *Queen Lucia*, 1920, p.18.
34. William Turnbull: 'Something Better in Design', in the *Furnishing Trades Organiser*, May 1923, p.350
35. 'The Trend of Design in Modern Fabrics' – an interview with Rex Silver in *The Christian Science Monitor*, 4 May 1923.
36. *Ideal Home*, March 1928, p.212.
37. *ibid.*, p.304.
38. Nikolaus Pevsner in *The Architectural Review*, June 1936, p.295.
39. A letter from Florence Cook to Miss Mary Peerless on the death of Rex Silver, 24 September 1965 (in the Silver Studio Collection, Middlesex Polytechnic).
40. *The Studio*, Vol. IX, pp.274–5.

The Silver Family

by William Ruddick

In our period of mass mobility and smaller families, it is hard to recreate the atmosphere of a later Victorian middle-class community, linked by a complex network of family relationships, personal friendships, religious affiliations and business connections. One or two Victorian communities such as that at Bedford Park have recently been studied and such celebrated artistic groups as the Pre-Raphaelites have always been well known: but unless a group consisted of highly-gifted individuals working within a single art form, or a mixed group of cultured people living in prime artistic surroundings, it has generally been almost entirely forgotten. Yet Victorian London was full of groups of cultured and artistic middle-class people whose lives and work have generally received little attention hitherto.

The old Charlotte Street community of artists, craftsmen and émigré teachers did much to foster the genius of Pre-Raphaelitism. The new middle-class suburbs which developed as a consequence of improved public transport after about 1870 encouraged a migration of artists and designers whose parents had, in many cases, belonged to the closely-knit old inner-city artisan and craftsman class. London's growing market for furniture and decoration of good quality, together with improved opportunities for education in applied art and design within the metropolis, also steadily drew in new talent from the provinces.

The last quarter of the nineteenth century sees the emergence into prominence and respectability of a new class of artistic designers. In this respect, Arthur Silver's tragically short life story is characteristic of his time and place. He was born at Reading, on 24 January 1853, into the old shopkeeper-craftsman class. His father, James Silver, offered a range of services which speaks for the lack of consequence (and of financial return) attached to any of them individually at this period. He was 'upholsterer, cabinet-maker, paper-hanger, estate agent, valuer, undertaker and agent to the Eagle Life Office'. James Silver prospered in the course of time and was twice Mayor of Reading. But with the steady growth of population (and wealth) in Victorian England, no one individual needed to go on combining so many occupations in order to make a living: indeed, as a consequence of the growth of public interest in and awareness of the domestic arts, the upholstery and cabinet-making sector alone was able to give employment to two branches of James's family. The firm of H. Silver specialised in furniture and domestic furnishings in Reading throughout Rex Silver's lifetime, and at the same time Arthur Silver and his sons were able to specialise in designing the materials requisite for the upholsterer's and the paperhanger's crafts.

Arthur Silver's education shows a fruitful combination of old and new features which it would have been impossible to achieve before the middle of the nineteenth century. At Reading School of Art he benefited from the Government-sponsored scheme for education in design for industry laid down by Sir Henry Cole. On completing his studies (at which surviving notebooks show that he was enterprising and diligent) he was articled in traditional fashion to the well-known and eclectic London designer H. W. Batley. By the time he was twenty-five Arthur was financially secure enough to marry. His bride was Isabella Walenn, the daughter of an ingenious and alert-minded gentleman who had had some success as an inventor and was scientist enough to work for a time as an assistant to Lord Kelvin: he eventually became a technical advisor to the Patents Office in London.

The Walenn family was large, closely-knit and artistically gifted. Several of Arthur's brothers and sisters-in-law achieved distinction in their various fields. Herbert Walenn was Professor of Cello at the Royal Academy of Music for fifty years: Sir John Barbirolli was one of his pupils. Gerald Walenn was the first Professor of Violin at the Sydney Conservatoire. Arthur Walenn was a noted provincial singing teacher, particularly in the West Country. Frederick Walenn was a painter: he started the St John's Wood Art School. The girls, too, were enterprising. 'Unless Miss Ellie Walenn will be Head, we shall never have a Junior House', one of the founders of Roedean is reputed to have declared. When the Junior House was completed, the Silver Studio designed its curtains and soft furnishings. Dorothea Walenn taught the violin at St Paul's Girls' School for many years.

Arthur Silver's bride, Isabella Walenn, shared her family's interest in music, singing for many years with the Royal Choral Society. Before her marriage she spent two years in Budapest, living as their daughter's friend and companion with a noble Hungarian family. She is remembered as being ever-gracious, graceful, exceptionally sympathetic to a wide circle of friends, and very kind to the young.

The birth of Arthur Silver's son Reginald (Rex) in 1879 was followed by those of Arthur (1880), Harry (1881), Christine (1883) and Ellen Margerine (1886). The children grew up happily, surrounded by books and artistic objects. From an early period Rex and Harry, who were educated at the Godolphin School, Hammersmith, numbered the sons of design and business colleagues of their father (such as Lancelot Crane and Stacy Aumonier) among their friends.

Both Rex and Harry Silver went from school into the family business. Rex had the benefit of about a year's training from his father, and though he had wanted to become a professional artist he clearly felt he had no alternative but to accept the rôle of business manager of the Studio immediately upon Arthur Silver's death. Harry was trained in design by Harry Napper and other members of his father's excellent design team. From 1900, when Rex was twenty-one, he and Harry exercised full control over the Studio's affairs, with Rex as business manager and Harry as the firm's artistic director (though obviously to a considerable extent they shared ideas and decisions about artistic policy). Harry's carefully-considered decision to ease the financial problems of the Studio by withdrawing from the business during a very difficult period in the First World War was deeply regretted by Rex. It left him with the double responsibility for business and artistic supervision, though Harry was always ready to give help of many different kinds:

for the rest of Rex's life he and Harry met as often as possible for informal discussion of the Studio's affairs and future policy.

Their brother Arthur Silver was the odd man out in the Silver household in that he never expressed artistic interests. He went to South Africa in the Boer War, was awarded the MC in the First World War, and worked in Canada and Australia. But unfortunately he was stricken by Parkinson's Disease in mid-career and was an invalid for many years.

Christine Silver became an actress, the original Nibs in *Peter Pan*, the original Fanny in Shaw's *Fanny's First Play* and Titania in Granville-Barker's celebrated production of *A Midsummer Night's Dream*. She had a long and successful career, working also in films and television before her death in 1960.

Ellen Margerine Silver (who was always known as 'Baba') trained as a pianist as a fellow-student of Myra Hess and Irene Scharrer. Unfortunately she died early, of pneumonia, in January 1906. Her mother, Arthur Silver's widow Isabella Walenn, lived till 1936 and is the subject of innumerable friendly enquiries in letters to Rex from friends and business colleagues.

The Silvers and Walenns were a united and happy group, but Arthur Silver was also fortunate in the range and closeness of his friends. Patchy documentation makes it impossible to say how early Arthur became acquainted with several of the leading designers of the last twenty years of the nineteenth century, but it is clear from surviving letters that by the early 1890s several important friendships were well established and, indeed, close.

Perhaps Arthur's closest friendship was with the first editor of *The Studio*, Gleeson White. An examination of the early numbers of *The Studio* shows that Gleeson White went to some trouble to publicise his friend's designs and business activities. An interesting interview with Arthur appears in *The Studio*, Vol. III (1894) and Gleeson White wrote the catalogue for Arthur's exhibition of stencil designs at Rottman and Co. in 1896. Gleeson White was probably instrumental in securing the invitation for Arthur to lecture on 'The Modern Stencil and its Application to Interior Decoration' before the Architectural Association in February 1896. The friendship between the two men was based upon a thorough agreement concerning artistic principles. When Arthur died, Gleeson White wrote to Rex Silver that 'your dear father at times liked to discuss his designs with me' and went on 'I owe so much to him, and feel so heavily the loss of my most loyal friend.'

A less close friend, but one who obviously thought highly of Arthur Silver as a designer and lost no opportunity to advance his career, was Walter Crane. Little correspondence survives, but the records of the various societies with which Walter Crane was associated show that Crane proposed Arthur Silver as a member of more than one of them. In November 1893 Crane (a Past President) seconded a proposal that Arthur should become a member of the Arts and Crafts Exhibition Society made by his friend the architect Hugh Stannus (in all likelihood the proposal originated with Crane). Arthur does not seem to have wished to be elected, perhaps because growing deafness made the thought of committee work unwelcome, and perhaps also because he feared the demands that committee work might make upon his time: but he exhibited at the Arts and Crafts Exhibitions until his death.

In May 1895 Walter Crane seconded Arthur's candidature for the Art Workers' Guild (of which he had been Master in 1888 and 1889). Only three candidates out of a total of fifteen could be elected and Arthur's candidature was unsuccessful. Crane regretted the fact and was glad when Rex Silver became a member of the Junior Art Workers' Guild (then called the Art-Students' Guild) a few days before Arthur's death. Walter Crane's opinion of Arthur was that he was 'an able and graceful designer and an amiable character'. The two families grew close through the friendship of their children and correspondence continued for several years, but Arthur's death brought real professional relations to an end.

Other leading designers of the age were known by the Silvers to a lesser degree. As is to be expected of a designer who began independent work about 1880, Arthur Silver was at least acquainted with William Morris, besides being thoroughly familiar with his work. Later correspondence with Rex Silver indicates that Arthur knew C. F. A. Voysey personally, as well as being an admirer of his designs. But here again direct evidence in the form of surviving correspondence is lacking.

What is clear, however, is that Arthur also built up a wide and often very friendly relationship with the best and most forward-looking manufacturers of his day. The letters of condolence which several of them sent to Rex on Arthur's death (for example a series from Alexander Millar of Templeton and Co., the carpet manufacturers) show artistic respect for the work of the Studio, personal liking for Arthur and a desire to help his son. Rex continued to sell designs to a number of his father's most regular patrons until virtually the end of the Studio's active life, almost seventy years after Arthur Silver died.

The correspondence in the archives of the Silver Studio during Rex Silver's exceptionally long direction of the concern shows a definite change in character after the first few years. Arthur Silver had been a designer of quality building up a quality concern in a period of unprecedented public interest in the applied arts and household decoration. The number of Guilds, Societies and other bodies founded between 1880 (when the Studio opened) and Arthur's death in 1896, and the number of specialist journals founded after about 1890 makes more understandable the artistic commitment and energy implied by much of Arthur's and his friends' correspondence. Rex and Harry Silver began their careers at a time when the applied arts were still in a state of creative fervour. They shared the interests of the new generation of craftsmen and designers through their membership of the Junior Art Workers' Guild. But by about 1912 that lively body was finding itself in difficulties. Members such as the Silver brothers were too busy to keep in touch and a new generation of young designers interested in corporate activities was simply not coming on. Rex Silver and his friends corresponded on art and design matters in the opening years of the twentieth century. But by 1910, although family, friendly and (above all) sporting links might be maintained, the designers were settling into the role of design producers who kept up with and followed the markets, rather than original thinkers who tried to be in front of and stimulate (in order to improve) public taste. As *The Studio* itself shows, the full energy of the Arts and Crafts period was rapidly waning. The safe reliance on the reproduction of period styles which was to lie behind the bulk of the Silver Studio's (and everyone else's) activities for much of the rest of its life was clearly becoming dominant. Rex and Harry Silver largely relied upon each other for artistic stimulus and criticism. After Harry left the business, Rex was very much on his own. He determined the Studio's design activities, working closely with both his artists and the buyers for textile and wallpaper manufacturers. Their correspondence becomes almost a form of designer's shorthand: a brief notation of designs understood by all concerned. Designs might be excellent in themselves, but the time was past when manufacturer or designer felt impelled to stand back and think about more fundamental concerns than what might best be done in the present state of public taste and the conditions of the commercial market.

This is not to say that Rex Silver did not do his utmost to provide good designs. He attended trade fairs, visited the great British and French exhibitions (such as that in Paris in 1925), subscribed to new publications, collected materials and read avidly and was clearly very interested in every new attempt to improve standards of design. But his concern was that of an individual, working in a period lacking in any great artistic dynamism. His isolation was increased as other independent design studios closed and old friends either retired or died. By the time Rex himself died the Silver Studio was almost the last such organisation left in existence.

But if the upsurge in artistic energy which characterises Arthur Silver's period as an independent designer waned sharply and was absent for most of Rex's career, the story of the Silver family itself shows the middle-class artistic and professional character of the late-nineteenth-century Silvers and Walenns continuing in a remarkably consistent fashion. Designers, musicians, teachers and related professions continue to appear in the family right up to the present day.

Harry Silver married before Rex. His grandchildren follow careers in architecture and design.

Rex acted as head of the family until his brothers and sisters were grown up and had careers of their own. The letters show a characteristic Edwardian interest in sport and travelling, whenever time could be found for them in the midst of a great deal of hard work. In 1915 Rex married Ruby Orchard, the daughter of a man who had maritime and property interests. Ruby had herself had an education in craft work and was an accomplished metal and silverwork designer. Unfortunately she died only two years after the marriage.

In 1922 Rex married Sybil Peerless, an early friend (and distant relation) who had been widowed during the War. Her daughter Mary Peerless, who was ultimately to save the Silver Studio Collection from dispersal and find it its present home with Middlesex Polytechnic, demonstrates once more the closeness of the Walenn-Silver connections: she attended Roedean and went on to become a professional viola player and teacher. Harry Silver's daughters Erica and Gay were also pupils at the school and Christine Silver's daughter Barbara Sturgis taught English at Roedean for twenty-seven years.

If Rex Silver had not had the good fortune to enjoy excellent health until his middle eighties, it is doubtful whether the Collection could have survived in a state approaching completeness. Rex was very proud of his, his brother's and their father's achievement and in later years he delighted in showing the Studio to visitors. In his last years he began to be visited by the new school of design historians, who realised the significance of the Studio's survival. Had Rex died ten years earlier, however, it is doubtful whether any institution would have thought such a large mass of potential research material worth preservation.

Aside from the Silver Studio Collection's significance for art historians, it also offers much to interest the social historian. Rex Silver's pocket diaries and a good many of the letters enable us to form a clear picture of the domestic life and social habits of a London professional-class family from the early 1890s onwards. The picture is particularly clear in the 1930s and during the Second World War period. Rex and Sybil Silver were keen cinema and theatre goers (always attending plays in which Rex's sister Christine performed) and as Mary Peerless's musical education advanced they became regular concert goers. There are also details of the expansive English summer holidays of the time. The Silver Studio correspondence may show the general loss of artistic vitality which affected the applied arts in England generally after the first decade of this century. As a social record, however, it expands and grows more vivid with the passing of time.

Bibliography

Surprisingly little has been written on the Silver Studio or the designers who worked there. The following is a list of works which include at least a brief mention of the Studio, although journals and catalogues frequently illustrated textiles and wallpapers from Silver Studio designs without crediting the source of the design – the exceptions being the early *Studio* decorative art year books and *Der Moderne Stil*.

'A studio of design. An interview with Mr A. Silver'. *The Studio*, Vol. III, 1894, pp.117–22.

Practical Designing, edited by Gleeson White, 1894. Includes articles by Arthur Silver on 'Designing for Woven Fabrics', 'Printed fabrics', and 'Floorcloths'.

'Stencilled Fabrics for Decorative Wallhangings', *The Studio*, Vol. v, 1895, pp.181–5.

'The Modern Stencil and its Application to Interior Decoration': a lecture by Arthur Silver reprinted in *The Building News*, 1896, pp.305–7, *The Architect*, February 1896, pp.141–4, and *The Journal of Decorative Arts*, June 1896, pp.152–5.

'The Trend of Design in Modern Fabrics': an interview with Rex Silver in *The Christian Science Monitor*, 4 May 1923.

A History of English Wallpaper by A.V.Sugden and J.L.Edmondson, Batsford, 1925.

A Survey of British Industrial Arts by H.G.Dowling, F.Lewis Limited, 1935.

British Textile Designers of Today by H.G.Hayes Marshall, F.Lewis Limited, 1939.

British Designers and Their Work, Series 1, edited by Frank Lewis, F.Lewis Limited, 1941.

'End of the Silver Studio', *Country Life*, Vol. CXL, 1966, pp.1595–6.

Liberty's 1875–1975, Victoria and Albert Museum exhibition catalogue, edited by Shirley Bury, 1975.

Wallpapers by Brenda Greysmith, Studio Vista, 1976.

'New light on the Liberty Metalwork Venture' by Shirley Bury, *The Bulletin of the Decorative Arts Society*, 1976.

'The Silver Studio Collection and the History of Design' by Joseph Darracott, *Connoisseur*, Vol. 170, No.684, 1969, pp.84–6.

The Designs of Archibald Knox by A.J. Tilbrook, Ornament Press, 1976.

Arts and Crafts in Britain and America by Isabelle Anscombe and Charlotte Gere, Academy Editions, 1978.

'The Silver Studio's Contribution to British Wallpaper Design 1890–1930' by Mark Turner, in *Design History: Fad or Function*, Design Council, 1978.

Three Generations of a Family Textile Firm by Jocelyn Morton, 1971.

Chronology

1853	Arthur Silver born at Reading
1869	Attended Reading School of Art
1872	Apprenticed to H.W.Batley
1878	Married Isabella Walenn and rented 132 Coningham Road, Shepherds Bush
1879	Rex Silver born
1881	Harry Silver born
1884	Arthur Silver bought 84 Brook Green, Hammersmith Edmund Hunter apprenticed to the Silver Studio
1886	Studio added to 84 Brook Green
1887	Arthur Silver designed Queen Victoria's portrait medal
1888	Woollams Wallpaper *The Fig* designed by Arthur Silver exhibited at the first Arts and Crafts Exhibition Arthur Silver subscribed to S.Bing's magazine *Artistic Japan*
1889	Arthur Silver rented 4 Haarlem Road, Brook Green as additional studio premises Exhibited two designs for cretonnes at the second Arts and Crafts Exhibition. Wallpapers designed by Arthur Silver exhibited at *The Exposition Universelle*, Paris
1890	Exhibited three designs at the third Arts and Crafts Exhibition
1893	Arthur Silver gave up No.4 Haarlem Road and bought No.3 Haarlem Road for Studio premises Exhibited seven objects at the Arts and Crafts Exhibition, including *The Days of Creation* gesso panel executed by Harry Napper Harry Napper and John Illingworth Kay working at the Silver Studio Commissioned by Warner and Sons Ltd, to execute designs for woven silks for the marriage trousseau for Princess May of Teck Woollams wallpapers designed by the Silver Studio exhibited at *The World's Columbian Exposition*, Chicago Arthur Silver became a member of the Royal Society of Arts
1894	Arthur Silver interviewed on the Silver Studio by *The Studio* magazine (Vol. III, pp.117–22). Contributed three sections (on designing for Printed Textiles, Woven Textiles and Floorcloths) to Gleeson White's *Practical Designing* The Studio exhibited fifteen designs for woven silks at *The National Silk Textile Exhibition*
1895	Stencil decorations by the Studio exhibited at Rottmann & Co. Interviewed by *The Studio* magazine in an article entitled 'Stencilled Fabrics for Decorative Wallhangings' (*The Studio*, Vol v, pp.181–5)
1896	Rex Silver a member of the Junior Art Workers' Guild Arthur Silver lectured to the Architectural Association on *The Modern Stencil and its Application to Interior Decoration* The Studio exhibited seven designs for textiles and wallpaper at the Arts and Crafts Exhibition. Arthur Silver died on 28 October. Harry Napper became design manager of the Studio

1898	The Studio produced some of the first designs for Liberty's new *Cymric* range of silver Harry Napper left the Studio and was succeeded by J. R. Houghton as design manager
1900	*The Conister* silver candlestick produced by Liberty from a design by Archibald Knox illustrated in *The Studio* magazine, Vol. XIX, p.127, as the work of Rex Silver
1901	Rex Silver and his brother Harry took over the complete management of the Silver Studio
1902	Designs by Harry Napper and the Silver Studio exhibited at the International Exhibition of Modern Art at Turin
1909	Rex and Harry began a new stencilling venture at the Studio
1912	Rex sold No.3 Haarlem Road and bought the Corner House, 1 Haarlem Road, Brook Green, Hammersmith to use as a studio
1914	Rex and Harry exhibited textile designs at the Arts and Crafts Exhibition in Paris
1915	Rex Silver married Ruby Orchard and joined the DIA
1916	Harry Silver left the Silver Studio to join the Army
1917	Rex's wife died. Rex worked for the Ministry of National Service The Silver Studio closed for one year
1922	Rex Silver married Sybil Peerless
1923	Rex interviewed by *The Christian Science Monitor*
1925	Rex Silver visited the Paris Exposition Internationale des Arts Décoratifs et Industriels Modernes with the Design and Industries Association
1930	Rex joined the Society of Industrial Artists and Designers
1935	Textiles and wallpapers from Silver Studio designs exhibited at the exhibition of British Art in Industry at the Royal Academy Rex made a fellow of the Royal Society of Arts Textiles from Silver Studio designs illustrated in Henry G. Dowling's *A Survey of British Industrial Arts* published by Frank Lewis, Plates lvi and li
1936	Isabelle Silver (Arthur's widow) died Rex interviewed by Nikolaus Pevsner for his series 'The Designer in Industry' published in *The Architectural Review*. Rex became a member of the National Register of Art Designers
1939	Designs by the Silver Studio illustrated in H.G. Marshall's *British Textile Designers of Today* published by Frank Lewis
1941	An article on Rex Silver published in *British Designers and Their Work*, Series 1, edited by Frank Lewis
1945	Silver Studio wallpaper of 1928 included in the exhibition of Historical and British Wallpapers, at the Suffolk Galleries (cat. No.181)
1952	Textiles from designs by Arthur Silver and Harry Napper included in the Victorian and Edwardian Decorative Arts Exhibition at the Victoria and Albert Museum
1963	Silver Studio closed
1965	Rex Silver died
1967	The Silver Studio contents were given to Hornsey College of Art (now part of Middlesex Polytechnic) by Miss Mary Peerless, Rex Silver's step-daughter

CATALOGUE

The Silver Family and Friends

Notes on Catalogue Entries

The following sequence has been observed for each catalogue entry:
Title, followed by *Dimensions*, followed by *Medium*, followed by *Inscription*, followed by *Date*, followed by *Description*.

All dimensions are in centimetres, height before width.

Full Inscriptions have only been given where these contain particularly important information.

An asterisk preceding the illustration number indicates that the piece is illustrated in black and white.

4

This section is devoted to objects and pictures relating to the Silver family, their friends and the designers who worked at the Studio.

1

Portrait of Arthur Silver
51 × 40·5
Oil on canvas
Inscribed *F. Walenn 1900*
1900

Posthumous portrait of Arthur Silver by his brother-in-law Frederick Walenn

Lent by Peter Haxworth

2

Portrait of Arthur Silver
17 × 11
Pencil on cartridge paper
Inscribed *Sunday 3–5 p.m.* (in Rex Silver's hand)
1895

By Rex Silver

Lent by Peter Haxworth

3

Plan of the Studio extention to 84 Brook Green
48·5 × 66
Pen and wash on tracing paper
Inscribed *Lewin Sharp & Arpin, Archts/3 Duke Street/Adelphi WC/March 1886 No.84 Brook Green W/A Silver Esq/Proposed Studios*
1886

Lewin Sharp became a good friend of Arthur Silver's – Arthur designed a gesso finger plate for him in 1894 which was illustrated in *The Studio*. Arthur found that despite this additional work space, there was still insufficient room to accommodate the staff needed for his rapidly expanding Studio. As a consequence he rented 4 Haarlem Road, and subsequently bought 3 Haarlem Road, directly behind 84 Brook Green.

SE.498.1979

***4**

Sketch of a girl feeding a calf
24 × 16
Pencil on cartridge paper
Inscribed *Kathleen*
c.1895

Executed by Rex Silver, probably whilst a pupil of Francis Bate

SD.2107.1979

5

Watercolour of a cottage at Pinkney's Green, near Maidenhead
21 × 40
Inscribed *Stacey Aumonier/Copthorne/August 1902*
1902

Watercolour by Stacey Aumonier of the cottage at Pinkney's Green which Arthur Silver, and subsequently his widow Isabella, rented for summer holidays

Lent by Mr & Mrs William Haxworth

6

Two Views of the rear elevation of 9 Wellgarth Road, London NW11
each 8 × 13·5
c.1935

Rex Silver owned this house from 1926 until 1964

SE.605(a) and (b).1979

7

Photograph of Arthur Silver's children
13 × 17
c.1890

From left to right: Harry, Christine, Rex, Ellen (Baba), and Arthur

Lent by Mr and Mrs William Haxworth

8

Postcard photograph of Christine Silver
14 × 9
Inscribed *Miss Christine Silver*
c.1900

Christine Silver (Rex and Harry's sister) had a long and successful stage career, creating Phoebe in J. M. Barrie's *Quality Street* (on tour before the London opening), Nibs in *Peter Pan* and Fanny in *Fanny's First Play* by G.B.Shaw. She played Titania in Granville Barker's famous 1912 production of *The Midsummer Night's Dream* and her performance of Tess of the D'Urbervilles in an adaptation of Hardy's novel was praised by the author. Later she appeared in Emlyn Williams's *The Corn is Green* with Sybil Thorndyke (an actress with whom she loved performing) and in post-war years she went on to do work for the cinema and television. Her relationship with Rex was always close. During the Second World War Rex's diary shows that he regularly escaped from the worries of the Studio to attend matinees with Christine, or performances of the plays in which she was appearing.

SE.604.1979

9

Arthur Silver's memorial card
7·5 × 23
Inscribed *In Loving Memory/of Arthur Silver/of 84 Brook Green W/who passed away October 28th 1896/in the 44th year of his age/interred at Kensal Green Cemetery*

SE.494.1979

10

Christmas card to Rex Silver's brother, Arthur
14 × 12
Inscribed *To Arthur Silver/This masterpiece/is dedicated/Xmas 1899/By Me/Stacy Aumonier*
1899

SE.519.1979

11

Catalogue for the Guild of Decorators Syndicate Ltd
21 × 17
1907–08

H.W.Batley, to whom Arthur was apprenticed in the 1870s, was part of this syndicate, along with W.J.Paulson Townsend, Henry Poole and others. The catalogue was reviewed in *The Art Worker's Quarterly* in 1908.

SE.500.1979

Both Harry Napper and John Illingworth Kay were talented artists as well as designers. The following Nos. 12 to 16 are examples of some of their work. Both exhibited watercolours at the Royal Academy.

12

View of Bosham Harbour
31 × 46
Watercolour on cartridge paper
Signed *H.Napper*

Lent by Miss Mary Peerless

13

View of Bosham
32 × 46
Watercolour on cartridge paper
Signed *H.N.*

Lent by Miss Mary Peerless

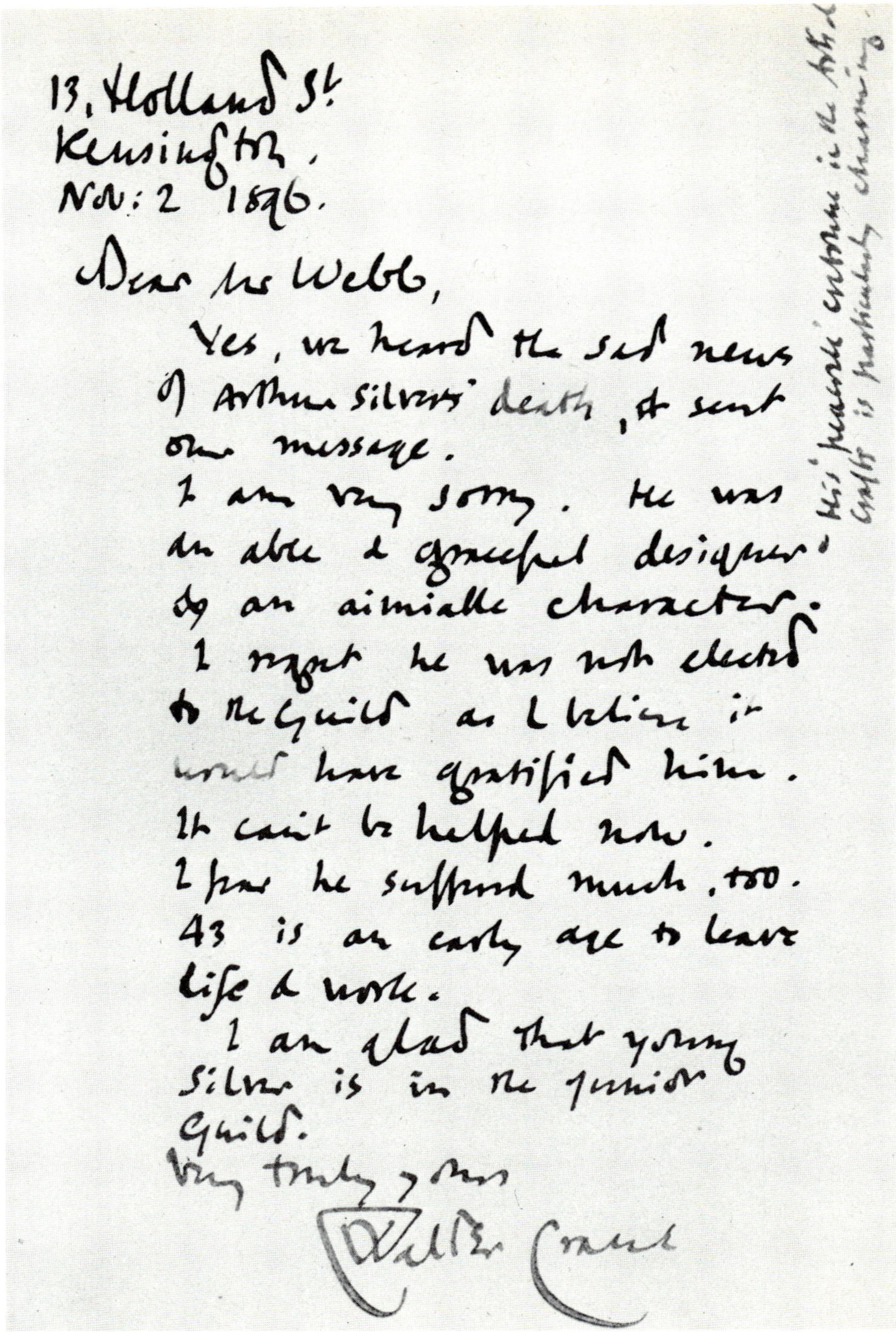

13, Holland St
Kensington.
Nov: 2 1896.

Dear Mr Webb,

Yes, we heard the sad news of Arthur Silver's death, & sent our message.
I am very sorry. He was an able & graceful designer & of an amiable character.
I regret he was not elected to the Guild as I believe it would have gratified him.
It can't be helped now.
I fear he suffered much, too.
43 is an early age to leave life & work.
I am glad that young Silver is in the Junior Guild.

Very truly yours
Walter Crane

His 'peacock' cretonne in the Arts & Crafts is particularly charming.

19

14

View of Itchenor from Bosham
22·5 × 31
Watercolour on cartridge paper
Inscribed *J.I.Kay/Aug.1900*
1900

By John Illingworth Kay

Lent by Mr & Mrs Neil Illingworth Kay

15

Landscape with fisherman
19 × 27
Etching
Inscribed *The Fisherman/J.Illingworth Kay*
c.1900

Lent by Mr & Mrs Neil Illingworth Kay

16

View at Pulborough, Sussex
30 × 21
Watercolour on cartridge paper
Inscribed *Pulborough/JIK/7·05*
1905

By John Illingworth Kay

Lent by Mr & Mrs Neil Illingworth Kay

17

Gesso casket
12·5 × 23
Inscribed *E.E.S./Her Box/JIK/18th June 1897*
1897

Made by John Illingworth Kay on his engagement to Emily Shiells

Lent by Mr & Mrs Neil Illingworth Kay

18

Two watercolour sketches of flowers
Various sizes
Watercolour on cartridge paper
Each signed *L.Aumonier*
c.1895

These are by Louise Aumonier, sister of Frederic Aumonier, Director of Woollams Wallpapers, and one of the Studio's best customers in the 1880s and 1890s. The Aumoniers were great friends of the Silvers. Louise was a talented designer in her own right, and seems to have sold a number of pattern designs through the Silver Studio. Her nephew was Stacy Aumonier, a well known novelist and journalist in the early years of the twentieth century, and a friend of Rex Silver.

SD.1467–SD.1474(a). 1979

***19**

Letter from Walter Crane to M.Webb
18 × 11·5
Dated November 2nd, 1896

This letter, written shortly after Arthur's death, is particularly useful as it gives us some idea of how he was regarded by his contemporaries. Walter Crane writes: 'He was an able and graceful designer and an amiable character . . . his peacock cretonne in the Arts and Crafts [exhibition] is particularly charming.' The guild referred to in the letter is The Art Workers' Guild. Rex had joined the junior branch of the Guild in 1896.

SE.522.1979

***20**

Dance card designed by Walter Crane
10 × 7
Inscribed *13 Holland Street/Kensington/May 6/1897*
1897

SE.520.1979

***21**

An invitation to Mrs Isabelle Silver (Arthur's widow) from Mrs Walter Crane
14 × 8·5
1910

Recto is a photograph of Mr & Mrs Walter Crane on camel and is inscribed *Garden of Allah/9.2.10* and, *verso*, is inscribed *Mistress Crane/bids you welcome to Old House/13 Holland Street W/June 30/9.30–1.00/RSVP*

SE.521.1979

22

Menu card for Smallman's Bakery
25·5 × 18
c.1890

Designed by Walter Crane

SE.536.1979

23

Christmas card
8·5 × 26
Inscribed *May/Christmas bring you Joy/and the New Year/Every Happiness/From Harold C.Bareham/to Mr R.Silver/1902/1903*
1902

Harold C.Bareham worked at the Silver Studio in the early 1900s and again from 1943 to 1963 as an outside worker.

ST.606.1979

20

21

***24**

Christmas card
21 × 29
Inscribed *Christmas Greetings/from Edmund and Dorothea Hunter/38D Market Place Hampstead Garden Suburb NW11/MDCCCCXXXV*
1935

Edmund Hunter was apprenticed to Arthur Silver in 1884, and remained in contact with the family until his death. He had started the St Edmundsbury Weaving works at Haslemere – later at Letchworth, and when the firm was taken over by Morton Sundour Fabrics Ltd, in 1928 to form the Edinburgh Weavers, Rex Silver was able to sell them some of his most important designs in the 1930s.

SD.513.1979

***25**

Christmas card from Ambrose Heal
24 × 14
Pen and watercolour on card
Inscribed *Christmas Greetings/from/The Fives Court, Pinner/A.H. INV EH.DEL.*
c.1920

The Silver Studio designed for Heal's in the early 1920s, and it is likely that Rex Silver had become acquainted with the Heals through the DIA, or the Art Workers' Guild.

SE.514.1979

***26**

Christmas card
27 × 12
Inscribed *Christmas Greetings from Edmund and Dorothea Hunter*
c.1930

SE.512.1979

***27**

Christmas card
23 × 15
Inscribed *Christmas/MCMXXXVI/To bring our Christmas Greetings/Edmund & Dorothea Hunter/ 15 Brim Hill/Hampstead Garden Suburb N2/ Speedwell 2448*
1936

SE.511.1979

24

***28**

Christmas card

18 × 11

Inscribed *Greetings from Alec, Margaret/and John Michael Hunter/Christmas 1937 Rails, Thaxted Essex*

1937

Alec Hunter was the son of Edmund Hunter and responsible for the Edinburgh Weavers first productions. He joined Warner & Sons Ltd, in 1932 and bought a number of designs from the Silver Studio. This card reflects his interest in Morris dancing.

SD.510.1979

27

25

26

28

***29**

Christmas card
19 × 27·5
Inscribed *with/all good wishes/from Dorothy and/Paul Woodroffe/Christmas MCMX/Westington/Chipping Camden/Glos.*
1910

Paul Woodroffe was best known for his book illustrations and designs for stained glass. He had become a friend of Rex Silver through his membership of the Junior Art Workers' Guild.

SE.509.1979

***30**

Invitation to Rex Silver from Mr & Mrs Harold Stabler
14 × 9
Inscribed *Mr & Mrs/Harold Stabler/request the Pleasure of your/company to see the/boat race./Mr and Mrs R Silver/RSVP to/34 Upper Mall Hammersmith/(Nearest station: Ravenscourt Park)*
c.1925–30

Rex Silver had met Harold Stabler through the Art Workers' Guild

SE.506.1979

***31**

Christmas card
22 × 16
Inscribed *Come let us be jolly/All green is the holly/and red is the berry/wake up and be merry/With Christmas Greetings/from/Mr & Mrs C H B Quennell/AD 1911/Four Beeches/Bickley, Kent*
1911

C.H.B.Quennell was a successful architect and interior designer, working c.1895–1930. He was a pioneer of light, panelled interiors, mixing homely antique furniture of different periods – very much Rex Silver's own taste. *The Studio Year Book* of 1908 illustrates and describes a house by him (pp.61–6) – Clive House, Roehampton, rather in the style of Ernest Newton; a dining room decorated by him is illustrated in *The Studio Year Book* for 1909 (p.21).

SE.508.1979

29

30

31

Part One: 1851 to 1890

With the work of most famous English pattern designers, it is possible to identify distinct stylistic periods. This has been done by Elizabeth Aslin for C.F.A.Voysey[1] and by Martin Eidelberg for William Morris[2]. For a number of reasons, the early work of Arthur Silver and the designers who worked for him cannot be so clearly catalogued. Firstly, with the exception of Edmund Hunter, who was apprenticed to the Silver Studio in 1884, we do not yet know the names of any of the designers who worked at the Silver Studio until the early 1890s. (Though it seems unlikely that Arthur Silver employed many staff in the 1880s.) Secondly, the early work of Arthur Silver shows a remarkable versatility. This is due in part to his apprenticeship to H.W.Batley from 1873 to 1878. Nowadays, Batley is best remembered for his sensitive Queen Anne Revival furniture designs of the 1870s, but in fact he made his early reputation as a Gothicist and was aware of the need for a professional designer to adapt to changing tastes. As a consequence, he taught Arthur to work in a wide variety of styles (as his sketch books from the mid 1870s reveal) and for a wide variety of media, which included carpets, furniture and plasterwork as well as textiles and wallpaper. This versatile approach is fully revealed in the objects in this section.

Yet while most of the work in this section is immediately recognisable as belonging to the 1870s and 1880s, either through subject matter or colour, no definite pattern of stylistic development emerges.

Quite a number of designs are clearly influenced both by William Morris chintzes of the early 1870s and by Arthur's own study of seventeeth- and eighteenth-century textiles in the Victoria and Albert Museum. A number of designs from the mid 1800s onwards use Japanese decorative motifs and others show the influence of a number of prominent designers, such as Walter Crane, E.W.Godwin and Owen Jones. Most designs are executed in fashionable, subdued, 'aesthetic' colours. This would all suggest that Arthur was working for fashionable and avant-garde manufacturers. That this indeed was the case can be shown by the manufacturers listed in the studio day books from 1891 onwards, and by objects such as his *Peacock Feather* cotton for Liberty's of 1886–7. Arthur seems to have been understandably cautious at first, and whilst the Studio's work is not often conservative, nothing is more than gently fashionable. He succeeded, during the 1880s, in building up a good reputation with a number of important customers, including Liberty's, Jeffrey and Co, and Charles Knowles. This reputation gave him the confidence and encouragement to concentrate almost entirely on the production of avant-garde designs in the 1890s.

[1] Elizabeth Aslin on Voysey's Pattern Design in the exhibition catalogue *C.F.A.Voysey, Architect and Designer* published by Lund Humphries and Brighton Museum, 1978, pp.96–100

[2] Martin Eidelberg on 'British Floral Designs and Continental Art Nouveau' in *The Connoisseur*, February 1978, pp.116–24

32
Copies of designs from Owen Jones's *Grammar of Ornament*
22 × 18
1873

This page of ornament from Owen Jones's *Grammar of Ornament* was executed by Arthur Silver probably while still at Reading School of Art. He made frequent use of Owen Jones's work for his designs in the 1880s, particularly if required to produce something exotic such as a design for a Moorish Smoking Room.

SE.485.1979

33
Examination Certificate awarded to Arthur Silver
14·5 × 19
1870

Awarded by the Science and Art Department of the Committee of the Council in Education for Arthur's success in the freehand drawing and perspective exercises in their Second-Grade examination

SE.490.1979

***34**
Science and Art Department
Examination Certificate awarded to Arthur Silver for the Second-Grade examination in Geometry.
14·5 × 20
1872

SE.491.1979

***35**
Science and Art Department Examination Certificate in Vegetable Anatomy (Elementary Stage)
23 × 16
1872

Arthur gained a second-class pass. The certificate is signed with a printed signature of Henry Cole, Secretary.

SE. 492.1979

***36**
Science and Art Department Examination (Second Grade)
38 × 28
1873

Certificate states that Arthur Silver had successfully passed his Second-Grade examination in the following subjects – Freehand Drawing, Practical Geometry, Linear Perspective and Model Drawing.

SE.493.1979

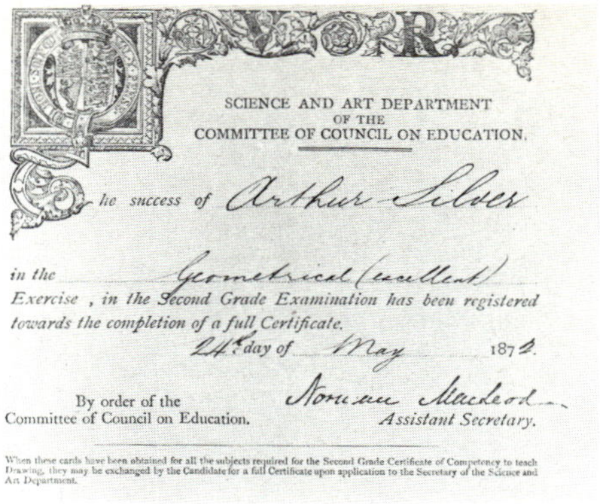
SCIENCE AND ART DEPARTMENT
OF THE
COMMITTEE OF COUNCIL ON EDUCATION.

The success of Arthur Silver
in the Geometrical (excellent)
Exercise, in the Second Grade Examination has been registered towards the completion of a full Certificate.
24th day of May 1872.

By order of the Committee of Council on Education.
Norman Macleod
Assistant Secretary.

When these cards have been obtained for all the subjects required for the Second Grade Certificate of Competency to teach Drawing, they may be exchanged by the Candidate for a full Certificate upon application to the Secretary of the Science and Art Department.

34

37
Sketch book
18 × 25
c.1875

This sketch book of Arthur Silver's dates from his apprenticeship with H.W.Batley, and contains designs for ceilings, friezes, and furniture. The styles are an eclectic mixture, including Gothic, Classical, French eighteenth-century, as well as naturalistic flower studies.

SE.486.1979

38
Page from Arthur Silver's sketch book
29 × 45·5
Pencil and watercolour on cartridge paper
Inscribed *8th/23.10.84/and 7th/16.10.85*
1884/5

SE.607.1979

39
Two pages of furniture designs from a sketch book by Arthur Silver
18 × 39
Pen and ink on tracing paper
c.1875

The right-hand page is signed and dated *A.S./6.74*. These sketches were probably executed whilst Arthur Silver was apprenticed to H.W.Batley. The left-hand design for a cabinet reflects the fashionable taste for elaborate French Second Empire furniture. The right-hand sketches reflect the growing middle-class interest in late eighteenth-century English furniture.

SE.527.1979

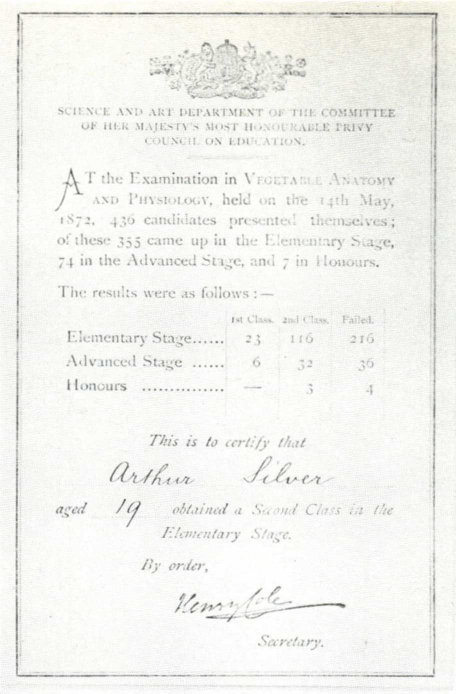
SCIENCE AND ART DEPARTMENT OF THE COMMITTEE OF HER MAJESTY'S MOST HONOURABLE PRIVY COUNCIL ON EDUCATION.

AT the Examination in VEGETABLE ANATOMY AND PHYSIOLOGY, held on the 14th May, 1872, 436 candidates presented themselves; of these 355 came up in the Elementary Stage, 74 in the Advanced Stage, and 7 in Honours.

The results were as follows:—

	1st Class.	2nd Class.	Failed.
Elementary Stage......	23	116	216
Advanced Stage	6	32	36
Honours	—	3	4

This is to certify that
Arthur Silver
aged 19 *obtained a Second Class in the Elementary Stage.*
By order,
Henry Cole
Secretary.

35

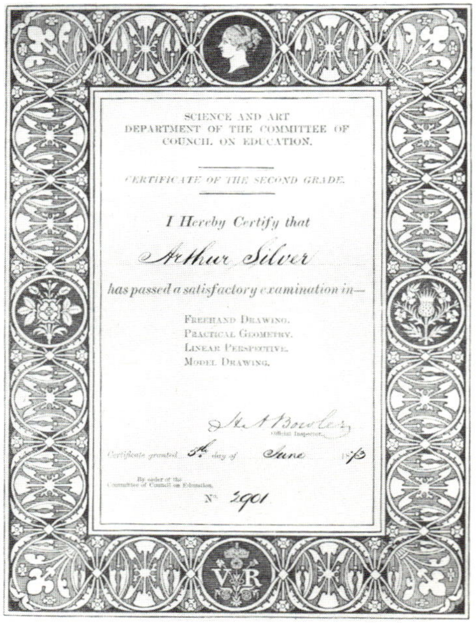
SCIENCE AND ART DEPARTMENT OF THE COMMITTEE OF COUNCIL ON EDUCATION.

CERTIFICATE OF THE SECOND GRADE.

I Hereby Certify that
Arthur Silver
has passed a satisfactory examination in—

FREEHAND DRAWING.
PRACTICAL GEOMETRY.
LINEAR PERSPECTIVE.
MODEL DRAWING.

Certificate granted 4th day of June 1873

No. 2901

36

40

***40**

Two designs for plaster ceiling decorations
each 32 × 24
Pencil on blue Ingres paper
c.1875

Elaborate neo-Louis XVI design for ceilings, probably executed by Arthur while apprenticed to H.W.Batley

SD.2108(a). 1979

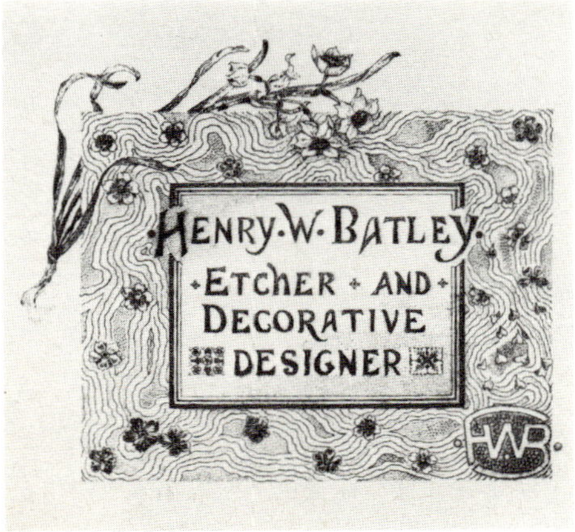

41

***41**

Trade card for H.W.Batley
11 × 15
Copper plate etching
Inscribed *Henry W Batley/Etcher and/Decorative/Designer/The Studio/74 Coomeragh Road/West Kensington/HWB*
c.1880

H.W.Batley doubtless introduced Arthur Silver to Japanese art, for he incorporated Japanese motifs into many of his designs during the 1870s and 1880s. Here he uses them on his own trade card.

SE.499.1979

***42**

Three examples of aesthetic movement trade cards
56 × 41·5 (mount size)
c.1880

The two lower cards were by T.Moyr Smith, an acquaintance of Arthur Silver's and an important influence on Silver Studio work of the 1880s.

SE.600.1979

The following furniture designs (43–8) are by Arthur Silver. Presumably he was taught to design furniture by H.W.Batley who became famous in the 1870s for his sensitive aesthetic furniture designs for Shoolbred's. It is likely that some of these designs were for the same firm, but at least one, a sideboard resembling Collcutt's work, was for the cabinet makers Marsh Jones and Cribb. Arthur probably stopped designing furniture shortly after 1880, and concentrated almost entirely on pattern designing. Particularly interesting are his elegant and elaborately inlaid neo-Adam designs for bedroom furniture, a style which was popular with those who admired elaborate French eighteenth-century furniture but were unable to afford it.

43

Sketch design for an overmantel
38 × 28
Pencil on cartridge paper
Signed *A.S.*
c.1880

The overmantel replaced the pier glass in English houses in the 1870s and 1880s for chimney-piece decoration. Most writers on interior design in the 1880s recommended them as a convenient way of displaying a large quantity of ornamental objects.

SD.171.1978

42

45

46

47

44

Design for a sideboard
27·6 × 34
Inscribed in pencil *7 ft 6 × 8.4 ins/2 trays/B range handles/No bevelling/cellarette drawer/Marsh Jones & Cribb/Leeds*
c.1880

Presumably this design was intended for the Leeds firm of cabinet makers Marsh Jones & Cribb, for whom H.W. Batley had designed Gothic furniture in the early 1870s

SD.172.1978

***45**

Design for a dressing table
12·8 × 17·5
Pencil on cartridge paper
c.1880

A revived interest in the furniture styles of the late eighteenth century developed in the 1870s. This particular design seems to be based on the work of Sheraton.

SD. 174.1979

48

***46**

Design for a wardrobe
21·2 × 16·2
Pencil on cartridge paper
c.1880

Note the neo-Adam ornamental detailing on this design

SD. 180.1978

***47**

Design for a towel horse, bedroom chair and commode
23 × 13·5
Pencil on cartridge paper
c.1880

SD.181.1979

***48**

Design for a half-tester bed
21·6 × 13·3
Pencil on cartridge paper
c.1880

Elaborate neo-Adam design

SD.176.1978

49 colour plate II

Design for a decoration of a door and wall
38 × 28
Pencil and body colour on paper
c.1885

Note the late nineteenth-century practice of dividing the wall into separate sections – a practice recommended by C.L. Eastlake in *Hints on Household Taste*, first published in 1867. The lowest section was the dado, the middle section on which pictures were hung was known as the filling, and the uppermost section was the frieze. With the demand for less demonstrative wall coverings and treatments after 1900, this practice gradually disappeared. The influence of Mackmurdo can be seen in the dado paper, and the frieze, with storks in roundels, reflects the work of Walter Crane. This work is a good example of design-conscious aesthetic decorating of the 1880s.

SD.3.1977

50

Design for a drawing room
28 × 38
Pencil on paper
Signed *A. Silver*
c.1885

This is a good example of an aesthetic interior. Note the use of Japanese decorative motifs and oriental objects.

SD.4.1977

***51**

Two designs for wallpaper
each 53 × 44
Charcoal and pastel on grey sugar paper
c.1880

Two exquisitely executed designs based on motifs from late eighteenth-century plasterwork combined with naturalistic flowers. They were probably intended for wallpaper. Opulent neo-eighteenth-century French and English designs were extremely popular during the late nineteenth century, especially for the decoration of the houses of the rich.

SD.1512–3.1979

52

Fragments of a dado paper and a filling paper
Various sizes
c.1880/1885

Both papers were taken directly from the staircase wall of a house in Putney. The lighter paper with the sprigged flower design was from the filling, and is a good example of a chintz design used for wallpaper. Both papers are printed by engraved copper rollers, (to produce a smooth surface for varnishing), probably by Lightbown and Aspinall.

Donated by Mr and Mrs Alexander Duthie

53

Portrait medallion of Queen Victoria
Diameter 22
Bronze
Inscribed *Victoria Regina/Annus Jubilaeus/* and signed *George Frampton 1887*
1887

An excellent example of Arthur Silver's remarkable versatility can be seen in his design for this charming portrait medallion of Queen Victoria, which was cast by the sculptor George Frampton and sold by Bellman and Ivey. The fact that Silver was commissioned to design the medallion shows how rapidly his fame had grown in the 1880s.

SE.516.1979

54

Press release for the Queen Victoria portrait medallion
21 × 13
1887

Produced by Bellman and Ivey, who sold the medallion

SE.517.1979

51

51

55

***55**

Photograph of Arthur Silver's portrait medallion of Queen Victoria
19 × 14
Inscribed *Her Majesty The Queen/G.G. Framption, Sc./Arthur Silver, Invt./Published by Bellman and Ivey, Sculpture Galleries, 37 Piccadilly, London W*
1887

SE.518.1979

56

Design for Arthur Silver's trade card
25 × 33·5
Charcoal on cartridge paper
Inscribed *A. Silver/Designer of Decoration/84 Brook Green/Hammersmith/Tapestry/Wallpapers/Carpets/Furniture*
1884

Design for Arthur Silver's first trade card for 84 Brook Green. Note the emphasis it gives to interior decoration rather than to pattern designing for commercial production. The use of the eighteenth-century cartouche as a basis for the design shows Arthur Silver being cautious and not risking the employment of an avant-garde aesthetic design.

SD.1076.1979

***57**

Trade card for Arthur Silver
9 × 10
Copper plate etching
Inscribed *A Silver/No 84/Brook Green/W/Designer*
1884

Probably both designed and executed by Arthur Silver, who was taught etching by H.W. Batley. The subject is a view of Brook Green from outside No.84, looking towards the Hammersmith Road.

SE.501.1979

57

58

Two designs for Arthur Silver's postal label
Inscribed *In Hoc Designo Vinces/From A. Silver/ 84 Brook/Green/W*
1885

This was probably designed by Arthur Silver himself, for he was fond of using ships in his designs

SD.482–483.1979

59

Printed postage label
9·5 × 13·5
Inscribed *In Hoc Designo Vinces/From A. Silver 84 Brook Green W.*
c.1885

SE.496.1979

60

Title-page *Chrysanthemums of Japan*
39 × 27
Inscribed *Chrysanthemums of Japan*
c.1885

Arthur Silver collected quantities of this type of material for use as source material for his designs. He also belonged to the Japan Society and subscribed to Bing's magazine *Artistic Japan.* Rex Silver found this material very useful in the 1920s when there was a vogue for oriental scenes as a subject for wallpaper and textiles.

SE.532.1979

61

Design for a wallpaper
60·5 × 56·5
Gouache and pencil on cartridge paper
Inscribed *361*
c.1885

This design is typical of the middle-class taste in the 1880s for large, demonstrative wallpaper patterns, and partly explains why late nineteenth-century interiors often appeared so gloomy. This particular design would have been for the wallpaper filling, viz. the area of the wall on which paintings would be hung. There would also be different papers (sometimes, but not invariably, related to the filling) for the lower part of the wall (the dado) and the uppermost part, above the picture rail (the frieze).

SD.1541.1979

62

Design for a wallpaper dado, filling and frieze
186·5 × 70
Charcoal and red crayon on detail paper
Inscribed *Victoria Regina 1837–1887/No 979*
1887

Probably intended for the wallpaper manufacturer Jeffrey and Co. for Queen Victoria's Golden Jubilee of 1887

SD.1440.1979

***63**

Design for a wallpaper
53·7 × 46·5
Watercolour and pencil on cartridge paper
Inscribed *844*
1888

This type of heavy, naturalistic design had been popular in conventional middle-class houses since the 1840s. Firms such as William Woollams hand-block printed many similar designs in the 1880s and 1890s.

SD.1525.1979

The following designs (64–70) show either the direct influence of the work of William Morris, or else, like Morris, show the results of Arthur Silver's studies of historic textiles in the Victoria and Albert Museum. Many designers working in the 1880s, such as Walter Crane and Lewis F. Day, were particularly interested in the rich, swirling designs of late Renaissance velvets and brocades. This interest is reflected in much of the Silver Studio's work in the 1880s, and in the series of photographs – The Silvern Series – of historic textiles from the Victoria and Albert Museum, which Arthur Silver sold to other designers and manufacturers.

***64**

Design for a wallpaper
42·2 × 52·8
Gouache on cartridge paper
Inscribed *561*
c.1885

SD.1527.1979

63

65

Design for a printed cotton
62 × 51·2
Gouache on cartridge paper
Inscribed *673*
1886

In this large and opulent design of *Opium Poppies* by Arthur Silver it is possible to detect early traces of the Silver Studio's Art Nouveau designs of the mid 1890s. Note the fashionable aesthetic colours, including sage green, dull pink and buff ground.

SD.1511.1979

***66**

Design for a wallpaper
51 × 51
Gouache on cartridge paper
Inscribed *709*
1888

Because William Morris pattern designs were very popular in the 1880s, Arthur Silver was frequently asked by manufacturers to produce adaptations, of which this is a good example

SD.1202.1979

67

Design for a printed furnishing textile
47·5 × 35
Gouache on tracing paper
Inscribed *No 794*
1888

Design, probably for a chintz, derives from Morris chintz designs of the late 1870s. Note that there are only two colours employed, which would suggest that this would be for an inexpensive textile.

SD.1283.1979

64

66

***68**

Design for a wallpaper
53 × 65
Watercolour on cartridge paper
Inscribed *1214*
c.1890

An important design, as it anticipates the richly coloured and vigorous Silver Studio Art Nouveau designs of the mid 1890s. The *Opium Poppy* was one of the most popular subjects for Silver Studio designs in the 1890s.

SD.1185.1979

***69**

Design for a printed cotton
48·2 × 56·7
Gouache and pencil on cartridge paper
Inscribed *906*
c.1890

This design, despite its dull colouring, also anticipates Silver Studio Art Nouveau of the mid 1890s. Notice how the chintz pattern is given a vigorous organic quality by the spiralling upward flow of the conventionalized poppies.

SD.1539.1979

70

Design for a dado paper
56.6 × 50·2
Gouache on cartridge paper
Inscribed *No.860 (6)*
1889

Opulent, heavy design probably inspired by eighteenth-century Spanish leather, which was very fashionable amongst the rich at the end of the nineteenth century as a wallcovering. This design was almost certainly intended for use as a paper for the dado, the lower section of the wall between the skirting and the filling.

SD.1535.1979

The following designs (71–88) have been loosely grouped together on the grounds that they are fairly typical, fashionable aesthetic-movement productions. Many are characterised by the influence of Japanese art and executed in subdued shades of green, yellow and brown. Some are strongly influenced by the work of important designers such as Walter Crane and Christopher Dresser.

***71**

Design for a printed textile
28 × 21·5
Pencil and charcoal on cartridge paper
Inscribed *No.424*
c.1885

Very dense design of swirling acanthus leaves and primrose flowers, much influenced by the work of Burne Jones and A.H.Mackmurdo. Probably by Arthur Silver.

SD.2103.1979

68

71

69

***72**

Design for a wallpaper and wallpaper frieze
53 × 53 and 26·5 × 57·3
Gouache, watercolour and gilt on cartridge paper
each design inscribed *706*
c.1885

Rich design in warm reds and gold for exactly the kind of wallpaper recommended by writers on middle-class interior decoration in the early 1880s. By the mid 1890s this type of design was no longer considered smart. Rosamund Watson wrote in 1897, in *The Art of the Home*:

'The "Art" wallpaper with its misbegotten sunflowers and poppies, its inane sham mediaeval dickie birds intertwined with geometric patternings, its livid complexion, now sour, now sallow, but ever revolting, they are all in the same tale. To be sure they have mainly ebbed out to the suburbs, but that is only so much worse for the surburbs.'

SD.1208–1209.1979

72

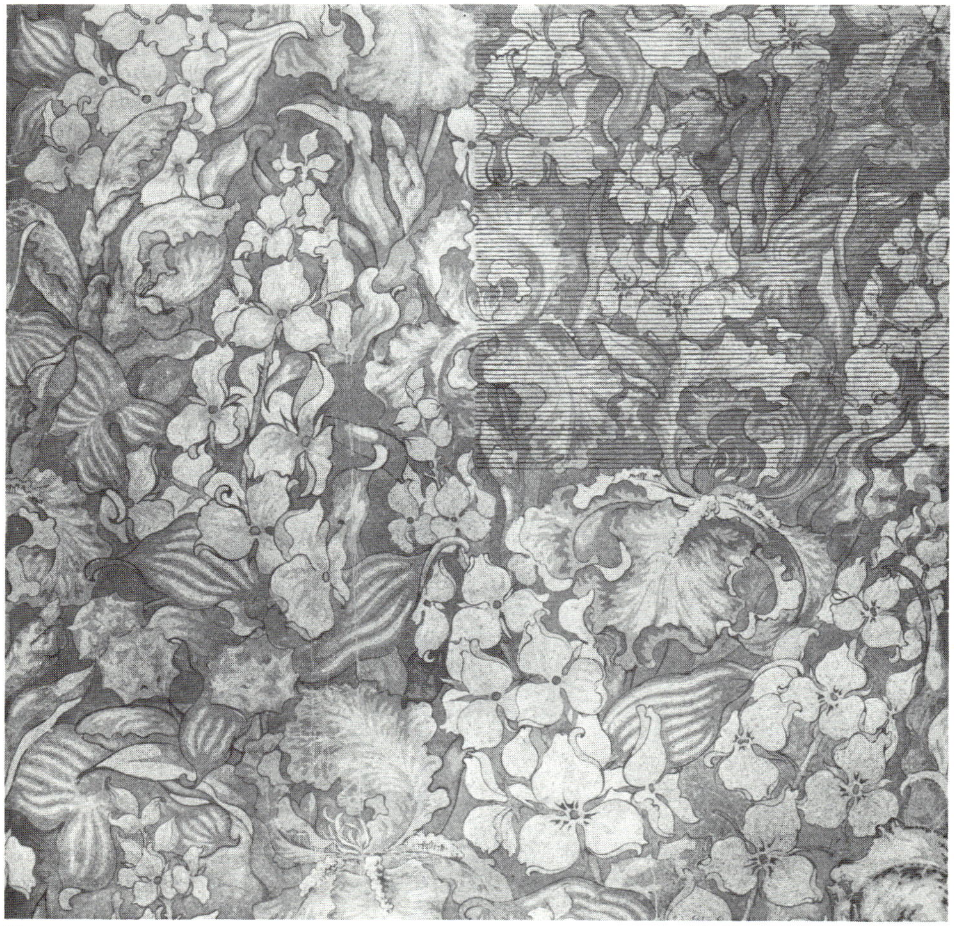

72

***73**

Design for a matchbox label
Pen and ink on card
Inscribed *1837–1887/Victoria Dei Gratia Regina/British/Empire/Match/Co/L.M/Hiawatha /73737*

An early example of Arthur Silver designing graphic material. Note how the matches in the lower corners have been drawn to resemble aesthetic sunflowers.

SE.504.1979

***74(a)**

Design for four panels of wallpaper
The Seasons
50 × 62·5
Gouache and pencil on cartridge paper
Inscribed *The Seasons*
c.1885–90

By Arthur Silver, showing the influence of Albert Moore

SD.1216.1979

74(b)

Design for a wallpaper panel
69·5 × 53
Gouache on cartridge paper
Inscribed *1040*
1887

Design intended for a wallpaper panel to occupy the space between the dado (which occupied the first three feet of the wall in an artistic house) and the frieze (which occupied the area above the picture rail). Note the influence of Albert Moore in the drawing of the figures set within classical frames.

SD.1475(b).1979

***75**

Design for a linoleum
36 × 26·5
Gouache on cartridge paper
Inscribed *No. 67*
1884

A quasi-medieval design doubtless inspired by the work of Owen Jones

SD.1222.1979

76

Design for a wallpaper frieze
36·5 × 66
Gouache and pencil on cartridge paper
c.1890

Design inspired by Persian Art and given delicate aesthetic colours

SD.1533.1979

BRITISH
EMPIRE
VICTORIA DEI GRATIA REGINA
MATCH Co
HIAWATHA: 73737.

73

75

74(a)

77

78

80

***77**

Design for a dado paper
41·5 × 49·7
Gouache on cartridge paper
Inscribed *620*
1885

An aesthetic design of squares containing peacock feathers and Japanese motifs, resembling E.W.Godwin's wallpapers of the 1870s

SD.1507.1979

***78**

Design for a linoleum
41·7 × 40·2
Gouache on cartridge paper
Inscribed *No. 71*
1884

This design shows the influence of Owen Jones in draughtsmanship and colour, and the aesthetic movement in the use of stylized sunflowers

SD.1223.1979

79

Design for a linoleum
23 × 23
Gouache on cartridge paper
Inscribed, *verso, 143*
1885

A Japanese inspired design of squares containing geometric motifs

SD.1221.1979

***80**

Design for a wallpaper
47 × 42·5
Gouache and watercolour and pencil
Inscribed *881*
1887

Design for a wallpaper based on decorative motifs from Japanese prints

SD.1198.1979

***81**

Design for a wallpaper
46·5 × 47·5
Watercolour, gouache and pencil on cartridge paper
Inscribed *No. 685*
1889

The design demonstrates clearly how Japanese art provided a major source of inspiration for English Art Nouveau

SD.1204.1979

***82**

Design for a wallpaper and frieze
53·7 × 29·7
Gouache and pencil on cartridge paper
Inscribed *822*
1887

Design for a wallpaper influenced by E.W.Godwin's wallpaper designs of the 1870s

SD.1520.1979

***83**

Design for a wallpaper
59·5 × 36·7
Gouache and pencil on cartridge paper
Inscribed *500*
1885

A sensitively drawn design for wallpaper in fashionable aesthetic colours – terracotta, sage green etc.

SD.1529.1979

84

Design for a wallpaper
45·5 × 53·5
Gouache on cartridge paper
Inscribed, in pencil, *505*
c.1885

Despite the naturalistic treatment of the flowers, note the organic quality of the design, and the fashionable aesthetic colours – terracotta, sage

SD.1532.1979

81

82

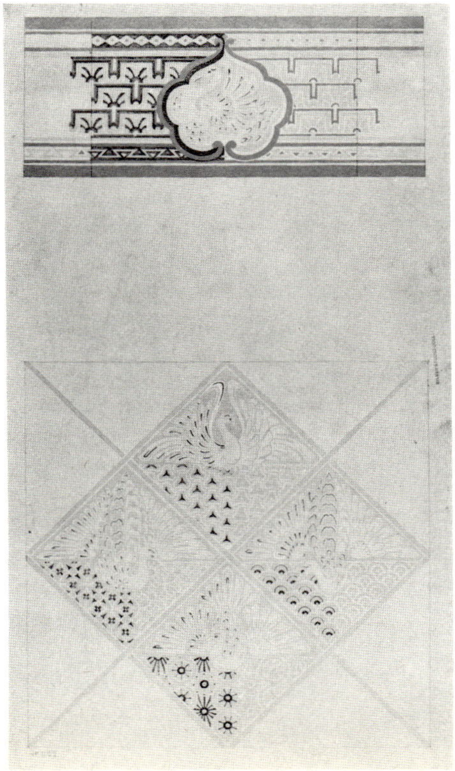

83

85

***85**

Design for a wallpaper
47·5 × 32·5
Watercolour and ink on cartridge paper
Inscribed *824/N.S/W.N.10*
1887

A simple briar-rose chintz design for wallpaper with aesthetic green and yellow colouring

SD.1285.1979

***86**

Design for a wallpaper
43 × 57·2
Gouache on cartridge paper
Inscribed *620*
c.1885

A typical aesthetic wallpaper design inspired by Japanese decorative art

SD.1528.1979

87

Design for a printed furnishing textile
45 × 63·5
Gouache on cartridge paper
Inscribed *No. 777*
c.1885

A delicate floral chintz design in red and gold on a pale primrose ground. This type of design is in complete contrast to the heavy period or naturalistic designs that were simultaneously available, and emphasises the very wide range of styles in which the Silver Studio worked in the 1880s.

SD.1540.1979

88

Sketch for a wallpaper design
43·6 × 26
Gouache on pencil on tracing paper
Inscribed *No. 1065*
1889

The combination of spiralling curves with marked formal qualities indicate that the designer was familiar with the work of Mackmurdo. (Doubtless Arthur Silver had become acquainted with the work of Mackmurdo through designing wallpapers for Jeffrey and Co., and perhaps had seen his work illustrated in *The Builder* in 1885.)

SD.1519.1979

86

89

***89**

Design for a label for The Silvern Series of Victoria and Albert Museum Photographs
12·5 × 18
Inscribed *The Silvern Series/No. . . ./SKM/ Reproduced/by/Arthur Silver/Designer/84 Brook Green/Hammersmith W*
1889

Label, probably designed by Arthur Silver, for individual photographs taken by Arthur Silver from the textile collection in the Victoria and Albert Museum. These were sold commercially, either as a source of inspiration for designers, or to be adapted by the Silver Studio to suit a manufacturer's particular needs. His choice of textiles to photograph provide invaluable information on those historic textiles which influenced the development of British Art Nouveau.

SE.484.1979

90

Silvern Series Photograph
56·5 × 53
1889

Photograph of a piece of eighteenth-century embossed Spanish leather

SE.532(b).1979

91

Silvern Series Photograph
62 × 72
Inscribed *Embroidery, 17th Century*
1889

This simple piece of embroidery, with acanthus scrolls and birds, is not very far removed from Voysey's work of the early 1890s

SE.533.1979

92

Silvern Series Photograph
72 × 62
Inscribed *Chair Seat, Venetian 17th Century*
1889

SE.534.1979

93

Silvern Series Photograph
72·5 × 62·5
Inscribed *Venetian*
1889

Photograph of a seventeenth-century Venetian brocade of a vigorous design of stylised pomegranates and flowers

SE.535.1979

Part Two: 1890–1910

In the 1880s, the work of the Studio was characterised by the very wide variety of styles produced, varying from neo-seventeenth-century damask designs to fashionable aesthetic productions for Liberty and Woollams. In the 1890s the Silver Studio was able to concentrate almost entirely on the production of Art Nouveau designs for wallpapers and textiles, with occasional essays into other fields, such as book covers and metalwork. By 1896, the year of Arthur Silver's death, the Studio was recognized as a major source of avant-garde pattern designs, selling not only to British manufacturers, but to French firms as well, notably Vanoutryve et Cie and Leborgne. Designs based on historic styles were produced only as special commissions, such as the Second Empire designs for Warner's silk tissues for Princess Mary, woven in 1893.

It was particularly in the field of wallpaper designs that the Silver Studio was most influential. With prices as low as a few pennies a roll, almost everyone could afford to use wallpaper. It must forever be to Arthur's credit that, despite his rapidly increasing fame in the 1890s, he rarely charged more than £5 for a finished design. For a two-colour wallpaper design, the cost could be as low as £2, so that the most competitive manufacturers, such as Lightbown and Aspinall and Potters of Darwin, could afford to use his services. As these firms sold the very cheapest wallpapers, Arthur Silver can be seen as directly responsible for making good pattern designs available to a wide range of people.

Arthur Silver's policy of supplying avant-garde designs was also encouraged by some enlightened manufacturers of printed furnishing textiles, such as Simpson and Godlee and O'Hanlon. Anxious to profit by the declining popularity of woven fabrics for upholstery and with design-consciousness no longer, in the 1890s, the prerogative of a few middle-class Londoners, these firms found it profitable to employ the services of well-known designers, and to advertise this fact.

Silver Studio designs, led by the work of John Illingworth Kay and Harry Napper, became increasingly organic and stylised up until 1900. Colours became richer and clearer, in marked contrast to the tertiary shades used for fashionable designs in the 1880s. Illingworth Kay's designs can usually be identified by their strong vertical emphasis, and often they have a marked landscape quality, derived from a careful observation of Japanese art. Napper's designs are distinguished by his use of flat, hard-edged flower and leaf motifs, and by his powerful and economic draughtsmanship. A possible source of influence on his style was Aubrey Beardsley's graphic work, which Napper may well have seen illustrated in *The Studio* magazine of 1893. Both these designers were constantly inspired by Voysey's patterns. (Voysey worked for many of the Silver Studio's customers and his work was frequently illustrated in contemporary journals.) Napper seems also to have influenced Archibald Knox's designs, both for metalwork and textiles. Knox frequently used stylised leaf motifs which first appear in Napper's designs of the mid 1890s. In turn, Archibald Knox's designs were imitated by Harry Silver when he began working for the Silver Studio c.1900. In particular Harry admired Knox's use of Celtic motifs in his designs.

Harry Napper left the Studio in 1898 and John Illingworth Kay in 1901. Harry Silver then became design manager until 1916. From 1900 to 1910 the Studio's Art Nouveau designs became increasingly controlled and formal. Abstract but tightly drawn botanical motifs on light grounds replaced the vigorous Art Nouveau of the late 1890s. Instead of bursting thistles and full blown poppies, there were tight little rosebuds and hearts arranged in vertical lines. It was during this decade that the Silver Studio sold large numbers of designs to European manufacturers, and it was this formalised, late Art Nouveau that had such an influence on the development of French decorative design in the early twentieth century.

Unfortunately English designers failed to see Art Nouveau as a style which could be further developed, and by 1910 it was virtually unsaleable. As a consequence, period styles once more returned to universal popularity. French period styles were given renewed impetus by the taste for Beaux Arts architecture (which resulted in such buildings as the Ritz Hotel, Piccadilly, by Mewès and Davis, 1906). The growing popularity of genuine and reproduction antique furniture led to an increased demand for appropriate furnishing textiles. From 1905 onwards, the Studio concentrated increasingly on the production of designs for textiles adapted from late eighteenth-century chintzes – motifs included Sèvres roses on ribbon trellis, or elaborate chinoiserie designs of magnolia branches and exotic birds. Designs such as these were the speciality of Herbert Crofts, who took over the design management of the Silver Studio after Harry Silver left in 1916.

94

***94**

Bookplate for Arthur Silver
13 × 10
Inscribed *Ex Libris/Arthur Silver*
c.1890

Illustrated in *The Studio*, Vol I, 1983, p.27

SE.497.1979

***95**

Design for Arthur Silver's trade card
20 × 30·5
Inscribed with a misquote from Keat's *Ode to a Grecian Urn: Heard sounds are sweet, but those unheard are sweeter*
c.1895

SE.483.1979

96

Sketch design for *The Floral Sea*
100·5 × 153
Charcoal on detail paper
Illustrated in *The Studio*, Vol. III, 1894, p.119
c.1890

One of the Studio's earliest and most publicized Art Nouveau designs, it was much influenced by the work of A.H.Mackmurdo, and by Arthur Silver's study of Japanese art

SD.2110.1079

97

Design for a frieze for *The Floral Sea*
91 × 149
Charcoal on detail paper
Inscribed *664*
c.1890

Although *The Floral Sea* design was sold for use as a printed textile, the existence of this frieze would suggest that it was originally designed to be used as a wallpaper

SD.2109.1979

95

98

***98**

Design for a trade card for Charles Knowles and Co.
30·3 × 50·3
Charcoal on detail paper
Inscribed *New Season's Patterns/18 × 18 or 16*
c.1890

Design, probably by Arthur Silver, for one of the Studio's most important customers in the 1890s. Charles Knowles and Co. was a wallpaper manufacturing firm who specialized in reprinting early nineteenth-century chintz designs from old blocks and who also made a point of using designs for inexpensive block- and machine-printed wallpapers from some of the country's leading designers. These included Christopher Dresser, C.F.A. Voysey and George Haité, as well as the Silver Studio. The firm was bought by A. Sanderson, in 1913.

SD.1132.1979

99

Design for a carpet
80 × 70
Gouache on squared paper
Inscribed *7311/N.S.*
c.1890

The Silver Studio was well known for its carpet designs in the 1890s, and Arthur Silver frequently sold designs to Templetons and Tomkinson and Adam (who also manufactured carpet designs by Voysey). Arthur Silver was trained in the techniques of designing for carpets and linoleum by H.W. Batley. Although this is a conventional Persian carpet design, Arthur Silver was capable of much more imaginative work, and was praised for his efforts to improve carpet design by Alexander Millar in an article 'Design in Modern Carpets' published in *The Journal of the Society of Arts*, 20 April 1894.

SD.1367.1979

100

Sketch design for a panel of wall tiling
97 × 61
Charcoal on detail paper
c.1890

Probably intended for a firm such as Pilkington or Maw and Co. who manufactured decorative wall tiling

SD.1416.1979

101

Sketch design for a panel of wall tiling
97·5 × 64·8
Charcoal on detail paper
c.1890

SD.1415.1979

102

Design for a gesso panel
29 × 22·7
Pencil on cartridge paper
Inscribed *No. 5*
c.1890

This delightful design reflects Arthur Silver's interest in the work of William Blake, Burne-Jones and Baroque Art. The draughtsmanship anticipates Continental Art Nouveau of the late 1890s.

SD.1554.1979

103

Design for a gesso finger plate
64·5 × 34·3
Charcoal on detail paper
Inscribed *1010*
c.1890

Like 102, this design reflects Arthur Silver's interest in the work of Edward Burne-Jones

SD.1166.1979

***104(a)**

Design for a cretonne
59 × 49
Gouache and pencil on cartridge paper
Inscribed *No 962B* and, *verso, 962/Cretonne/JC*
c.1890

This design is a combination of late eighteenth-century and Oriental influences, with sprays of heavy red camellias on a ground of vertical bamboo canes

SD.2009.1979

104(b) colour plate I

Design for a wallpaper
19·2 × 16·5
Pencil and watercolour on tracing paper
Inscribed *No 1421*
c.1890

By Arthur Silver and is the result of his close study of Japanese Art. The design of herons and swirling water would probably have been used for a filling paper for an aesthetic dining room. The rich colours used are in contrast to the tertiary shades popular in the 1880s for such designs.

SD.1392.1979

104(a)

105

***105**

Design for a dado wallpaper
88 × 51·2
Gouache on cartridge paper
Inscribed *No. 1063*
c.1890

This design was rather old-fashioned for the date. Note the use of cream terracotta and black, colours which were fashionable in the 1860s. The inspiration for the design probably came from Owen Jones's *Grammar of Ornament*.

SD.1400.1979

106

Design for a gesso panel
43·6 × 28
Orange, green and yellow crayon on detail paper
Inscribed *1251b*
c.1890

Arthur Silver was much interested in Italian Renaissance Art, and this design reflects this and in particular the work of Botticelli

SD.1155.1979

107

Design for a gesso finger plate
66 × 33·5
Charcoal on detail paper
Inscribed *1001*
c.1890

This design reflects Arthur Silver's admiration for the work of Sir Edward Burne-Jones

SD.1168.1979

***108**

Design for a cretonne
50 × 49
Watercolour on cartridge paper
Inscribed *888B*
1890

The vigorous organic quality of this design shows the influence of William Morris's designs of the early 1870s

SD.2049.1979

***109**

Design for a printed textile
57·6 × 49
Gouache on cartridge paper
Inscribed *No. 973.A.*
1891

This design reflects the popularity at this date of printed Indian cottons and silks. It may well have been intended for Thomas Wardle of Leek, who printed Liberty's Indian silks in the 1880s and 1890s.

SD.440.1979

108

***110**

Design for a trade card for John Line
24·6 × 32·5
Charcoal and watercolour on detail paper
Inscribed in charcoal *John Line and Sons* etc., and *verso* in pencil *London W.C. Oct. 29. 1891*
1891

Design, probably by Arthur Silver, for a very important customer of the Silver Studio. John Line and Sons had a cabinet-making business in Reading during the 1870s, and doubtless knew Arthur Silver's father. This trade card was intended for their first London wallpaper showroom which opened in 1892. By the 1920s they had become one of the country's most important wallpaper manufacturers, and the Silver Studio were still supplying designs to them in the 1950s. During the 1890s Voysey, Christopher Dresser and Lindsay Butterfield also supplied wallpaper designs to them.

SD.1136.1979

***111**

Design for a trade card for John Line & Sons
7·5 × 12
Pen and ink on card
Inscribed *9 Southampton Row, High Holborn, W.C. London Oct 23/91*
1891

By Arthur Silver for John Line's new London showroom

***112**

Copy of the *St James* wallpaper design by William Morris
22·5 × 13
Pen and ink on cartridge paper
Inscribed *Copied from the Art Magazine/M92/ The 'St James' Pattern/Designed by William Morris*
1892

This drawing is almost certainly by Rex Silver. Doubtless Arthur was training him in the way that he had been taught at Reading School of Art – by copying.

SE.523.1979

113

Design for a woven textile
37·5 × 38·3
Pencil and watercolour on tracing paper
Inscribed *No.1201*
1892

Design based on sprays of wheat, and in tertiary colours

SD.2102.1979

114

Design for a wallpaper
57·5 × 71·7
Watercolour on cartridge paper
Inscribed *1493*
1892

Design inspired by late eighteenth-century French ornament, doubtless intended for a wallpaper to be used with real, or reproduction French eighteenth-century furniture, or one of the more elaborate English styles, such as Sheraton. For those who could afford it, the taste for French decorating was consistently popular throughout the 1890s and early 1900s.

SD.1547.1979

***115**

Design for a wallpaper
72·2 × 60
Gouache and pencil on cartridge paper
Inscribed *1444*
1892

This design of hibiscus and other flowers, despite the good draughtsmanship, has a naturalistic treatment which resembles the popular wallpaper designs of the mid nineteenth.century

SD.1545.1979

109

TELEGRAMS "LINE SOUTHAMPTON ROW W.C."
OR "LINE READING"
JOHN LINE AND SONS
9 SOUTHAMPTON ROW HIGH HOLBORN W.C.
READING & LONDON
THE "JL&S"
ARTISTIC WALL AND CEILING PAPERS, BY HAND AND MACHINE
REGISTERED PATTERNS BY THE BEST DESIGNERS
& DECORATIONS IN RELIEF &c

110

Copied from the Art Magazine.
THE "ST JAMES'S" PATTERN.
Designed by William Morris.

112

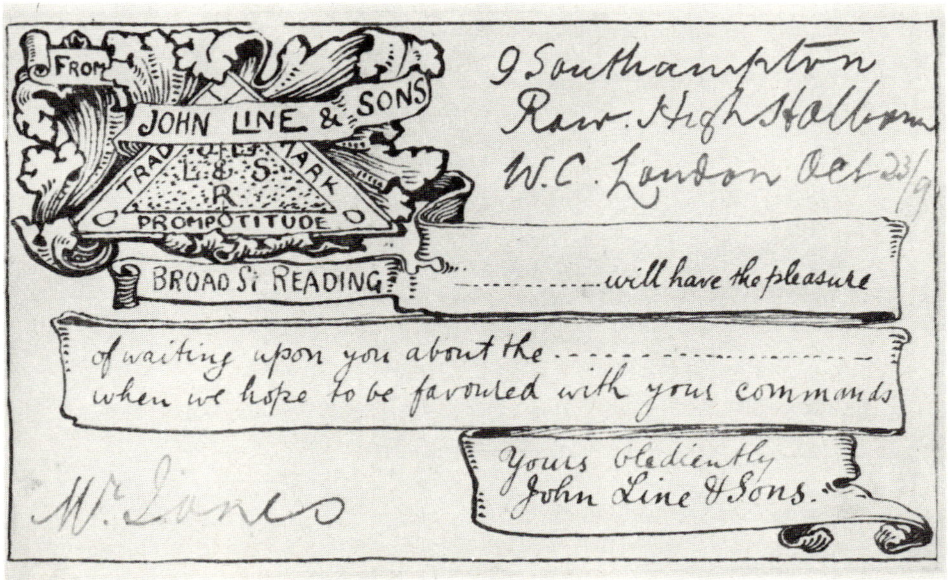
FROM
JOHN LINE & SONS
TRADE MARK
L & S
R
PROMPTITUDE
BROAD St READING
9 Southampton Row. High Holborn W.C. London Oct 23/9
will have the pleasure
of waiting upon you about the
when we hope to be favoured with your commands
Yours Obediently
John Line & Sons.
Mr Jones

111

115

116 colour plate IV, c

Design for a printed textile
54 × 54·2
Watercolour and pencil on cartridge paper
Inscribed *115C*
1892

Arther Silver continued to produce designs in the 1890s which were inspired by Japanese decorative art

SD.1524.1979

117

Design for a printed textile
30·7 × 35·2
Gouache and pencil on cartridge paper
Inscribed *1013*
1892

SD.1522.1979

***118**

Design for a wallpaper
61 × 44·8
Watercolour on cartridge paper
Inscribed *1579*
1892

This design continues the aesthetic tradition of the 1880s, in the use of delicate colours and Oriental influence

SD.1516.1979

119

Gesso panel
23 × 62
1892/3

This seems to be a trial section for Arthur Silver's large gesso panel *The Days of Creation*, which was executed by Harry Napper and shown at the 4th Arts and Crafts Exhibition in 1893 (Illustrated in *The Studio,* Vol II, p.24). The final panel was incorporated into the chimney piece of the drawing room at 84 Brook Green, and is now in the possession of Mr & Mrs William Haxworth.

SE.610.1979

118

120

120

120

***120**

Three trial sketches for the cover of *The Studio Magazine*
each 13·5 × 10
Pen and black wash on card
1893

Probably by John Illingworth Kay, who submitted five cover designs for a *Studio* competition in August 1893. His designs were highly praised and he was awarded an extra prize. (See *The Studio*, Vol. I, 1893, p.204)

SE.495.1979

121

Gesso door plate
63 × 31
c.1893/4

Illustrated in *The Studio*, Vol. III, p.153

This plate was executed for Lewin Sharp, the architect who designed the Studio extension to 84 Brook Green

SE.601.1979

***122**

Design for Arthur Silver's card for his city office
7·5 × 12
Pen and India ink on card
Inscribed *Mr Arthur Silver Designer has re-/moved his City office to/39 Warwich Lane EC/Friday 3–5 p.m. and by appoint-/ment. Messages forwarded to the/Studio: Postal Address/84 Brook Green W./January 23. 93*
1893

By John Illingworth Kay

122

It is an indication of Arthur Silver's fame by the 1890s that Benjamin Warner asked him to design the dress silks for Princess May of Teck's marriage to the Duke of York in 1893. Arthur had designed for Warner on several occassions before. He had produced a design for a silk tissue for the wedding of Princess Christian of Schleswig Holstein in 1891 (see 123) and a design for a silk for the wedding dress for Princess May's proposed marriage to the Duke of Clarence in 1892. (The Duke died shortly before the wedding was due to take place.)

Princes May's mother, the Duchess of Teck, had become president of the Ladies' National Silk Association and doubtless had encouraged her daughter to wear English rather than the more fashionable French dress silks. The designs that Arthur produced for these Royal silks are all in a delicate Second Empire style, and unlike any other designs produced by the Silver Studio during the 1890s.

Arthur Silver continued to be interested in designing for woven silks until his death, and in 1894 he exhibited fifteen designs for furnishing and dress silks at the Silk Association's second exhibition at Stafford House.

123

Design for a woven silk
51·5 × 49·5
Ink pencil and watercolour on tracing paper
Inscribed *Rose, Shamrock and Thistle, April 1891 1200/10/841/6*
1891

This is a design for a silk and silver thread tissue *Rose, Shamrock and Thistle* woven by Warner for the wedding of Princess Christian of Schleswig Holstein in 1891.

Lent by Warner and Sons Ltd (No.2943)

124

Design for the *Lily of the Valley* silk
55 × 36
Pencil and watercolour on tracing paper
Inscribed *Lily of the Valley and Orange Blossom 1891/Satin Ground faille stripes in damask and silver thread*
1891

This was woven by Warner at Spitalfields in 1892 for Princess May's intended marriage to the Duke of Clarence

Lent by Warner and Sons Ltd (No.2999)

The following designs (125–39) are for silks for Princess May of Teck's wedding to the Duke of York in 1893. The designs were all executed by Arthur Silver in 1892 and 1893, and woven by Warner and Sons Ltd at Hollybush Gardens, Spitalfields in 1893.

125

Design for a woven silk for Princess May's wedding dress
45 × 36
Watercolour and pencil on tracing paper
1893

Silver Studio design No.1306H

Lent by Warner and Sons Ltd

126

Design for a woven silk for Princess May's trousseau
45 × 43
Pencil on squared paper
Inscribed *Jasmine 1893*
1893

Silver Studio design No.1306I

Lent by Warner and Sons Ltd

127

Design for a silk tissue for Princess May's trousseau
46 × 41·5
Pencil and watercolour on tracing paper
1892–3

Silver Studio design No.1306D

Lent by Warner and Sons Ltd (No.1501)

128

Design for a silk tissue
38 × 35
Pencil, watercolour, silver point on tracing paper
1892–3

Silver Studio design No.1306E

Lent by Warner and Sons Ltd (No.1508)

129

Design for the *Esmond* silk tissue
41 × 35
Pencil and watercolour on squared paper
Inscribed *The Esmond*
1892–3

Silver Studio design No.1306C

Lent by Warner and Sons Ltd (No.746)

130

Design for a silk for Princess May's trousseau
39·5 × 28
Pencil and watercolour on tracing paper
1892–3

The Design is pasted to the original mount by Arthur Silver's postage labels

Silver Studio design No.1306G

Lent by Warner and Sons Ltd (No.1511)

131

Design for a woven silk for Princess May's trousseau
53·5 × 41·5
Pencil, watercolour and silver point on tracing paper
1892–3

Silver Studio design No.1306J

Lent by Warner and Sons Ltd (No.1510)

132

Design for a woven silk for Princess May's trousseau
44 × 46
Pencil and watercolour on tracing paper
1892–3

Silver Studio design No.1306

Lent by Warner and Sons Ltd (No.1507)

133

Design for a silk tissue for Princess May's trousseau
42 × 38
Pencil and watercolour on tracing paper
1892–3

Silver Studio design No.1306B

Lent by Warner and Sons Ltd (No.1509)

134

Design for *The Heather* dress silk
30·5 × 26
Pencil on squared paper
Inscribed *Heather 1892/1008/8/375/4*
1892

Silver Studio design No.1174

Lent by Warner and Sons Ltd (No.824)

135

Design for the *Iris* silk tissue
41·5 × 26
Pencil on squared paper
Inscribed *Iris 1892*
1892

This design shows a stronger aesthetic influence than is usual in Arthur Silver's designs for Warner at this time

Silver Studio design No.1178

Lent by Warner and Sons Ltd (No.731)

136

Dress silk
276 × 58
Silk and silver thread tissue
1891

Woven from Silver Studio design No.1062 by Warner and Sons at their factory in Hollybush Gardens, Spitalfields, for the wedding of Princess Christian of Schleswig Holstein in 1891

Lent by Warner and Sons Ltd (No.2943)

137

Dress silk
102 × 58
Silk and silver thread tissue
1892

Woven by Warner and Sons at Spitalfields from Silver Studio design No.1175. It was for Princess May of Teck's intended marriage to the Duke of Clarence in 1892.

Lent by Warner and Sons Ltd (No.2999)

138

Dress silk
30 × 34
Woven silk silver thread tissue
1893

Woven by Warner and Sons at Spitalfields for the wedding dress for Princess May of Teck's marriage to the Duke of York in 1893

Lent by Warner and Sons Ltd (No.W.426(a))

139

Dress silk
96 × 60
Silk and silver thread tissue
1893

Woven by Warner and Sons at Spitalfields from Silver Studio design No.1306(1). It was for Princess May's trousseau

Lent by Warner and Sons Ltd (No.888)

***140**

Design for a wallpaper frieze
53 × 126.5
Gouache on cartridge paper
1893

This design was bought in an altered form (without the figures) by Charles Knowles in 1893

SD.1201.1979

***141**

Design for a chintz
56·5 × 95
Gouache on cartridge paper
Inscribed *1280II*
1893

SD.1380.1979

140

141

142

***142**
Design for a wallpaper
83 × 58·5
Gouache on cartridge paper
Inscribed *1745*
1893

This design is by John Illingworth Kay. He frequently based his designs on Oriental landscapes, and his work is usually characterised by a powerful vertical emphasis.

SD.1184.1979

143
Design for a wallpaper frieze
125·5 × 57·2
Gouache on cartridge paper
Inscribed *1628*
1893

SD.1368.1979

There is no entry 144

***145**
Designs for a wallpaper
59·8 × 88·5
Gouache on cartridge paper
Inscribed *1665*
1893

SD.1396.1979

***146**
Design for a wallpaper
58 × 71·2
Gouache and pencil on cartridge paper
Inscribed *No.1584*
1893

SD.1546.1979

***147**
Design for a wallpaper
43 × 62·5
Gouache on cartridge paper
Inscribed *No.1706/W.P. Not Sold*
1893

By John Illingworth Kay

SD.2057(d).1979

***148**
Design for a wallpaper
57·4 × 49·5
Gouache on cartridge paper
Inscribed *No.1670.B*
1893

By John Illingworth Kay

SD.2048(a).1979

149
Design for a wallpaper
74 × 55
Gouache on cartridge paper
Inscribed *1806*
1894

By John Illingworth Kay

SD.1189.1979

***150**
Design for a wallpaper
88·2 × 57·7
Gouache on cartridge paper
Inscribed *No. 1785A*
1894

By John Illingworth Kay

SD.1235.1979

151
Design for the *Renaissance* wallpaper
30 × 28
Pen and ink on cartridge paper
Inscribed *1752*
1894

By John Illingworth Kay and bought by John Line

SD.484.1979

145

145

146

147

150

148

152

***152**

Design for a printed furnishing textile
26 × 20·5
Gouache and watercolour on cartridge paper
Inscribed *1389b*
1894

The aesthetic movement had encouraged a taste for delicate, sprigged textile designs from the early nineteenth century, of which this design is an example

SD.1420.1979

155

153

Advertisement for Rottmann & Co.
28 × 21·5
1894

This design was possibly by John Illingworth Kay, and dates from shortly before Arthur Silver's stencilling venture with Rottmann

SE.478.1979

154

Catalogue of Arthur Silver's stencil friezes
26·5 × 10
1895
Catalogue for the exhibition of Silver Studio stencil friezes held at Rottmann's in 1895, with an introduction by Gleeson White (11pp.)

SE.502.1979

***155**

Cover for a catalogue of stencil samples for the Rottman/Silver stencil exhibition
30 × 12
Distemper on woven jute
Inscribed *Rottman's/Silver/Studio Series/of Stencilled/Decorations*
1895

SE.602.1979

The following stencil decorations (156–61) were all executed by the Silver Studio in conjunction with Alexander Rottmann in 1894/5, and were first publicly shown at Rottmann's in 1895. The stencilling was carried out at the Silver Studio. Alexander Rottmann doubtless provided both money and materials. (His firm imported many different varieties of paper from Japan.) The venture attracted considerable publicity, including an article in *The Studio* (Vol. v, 1895, pp.181–5).

156

The *Richmond* stencil frieze
82 × 213
Distemper on Japanese grass paper
Inscribed *The Richmond/No 1202/ Stencilled at the Silver Studios/Rottmann and Co. Silver Stencil Series*
1895

The design, possibly by Harry Napper, is of stylized poppies in red and green, on cream grass paper

SW.1557.1979

157

The *Holbein* frieze
94 × 95
Distemper on Japanese grass paper
1894/5

Exhibited at Rottmann's in 1895. Illustrated in *The Studio*, Vol. v, 1895, p.181

SW.676.1976

158

Two trial sections of the *Mercutio* frieze
87 × 93
Distemper on Japanese grass paper
1894/5

Stylized trees and grass in blue and copper on cream grass paper, designed by John Illingworth Kay. The influence of Art Nouveau is apparent in the whiplash shape of the lower tree branches.

SW.1559.1979

159

The *Argosies* stencil frieze
72 × 106
Distemper on hand-made paper
1894/5

This was probably designed by Arthur Silver. Illustrated in *The Studio*, Vol. v, 1895, p.183.

SD.1426.1979

160

The *Romeo* stencil frieze
112 × 98
Distemper on Japanese grass paper
Inscribed *Rottmann and Co's 'Silver' Stencil decorations/The 'Romeo' No2042*
1895

Probably by John Illingworth Kay. Design of stylized tulips in browns and yellow on beige grass paper.

SW.1558.1979

161

The *Orchard* stencil frieze
83·5 × 66·7
Distemper on cartridge paper
Inscribed *No.187C/with final alterations/The Orchard*
1895

By John Illingworth Kay. Note the delightful colour scheme and simple design, anticipating Silver Studio designs of the 1900s.

SW.1560.1979

162

163

164

***162**

Complete scheme for a tiled wall
46 × 18
Gouache on linen
c.1895

This design of dado, border, filling, border and frieze was presumably intended for a manufacturer of wall tiles, such as Minton or Doulton

SD.1491.1979

***163**

Trial design for a trade card for Arthur Silver
30 × 23·2
Pencil and ink on detail paper
Inscribed *84 Brook Green W/Arthur Silver/Designer*
c.1895

Probably by Arthur Silver

SD.1147.1979

***164**

Design for a wallpaper frieze
85·5 × 42
Gouache on cartridge paper
Inscribed, in ink, *V.7*
c.1895

This design is by C.F.A. Voysey, and has been dated at c.1895 on the grounds that it closely resembles a design for a wallpaper frieze exhibited at the Arts and Crafts Exhibition of 1896 and illustrated in *The Artist* of 12 October 1896, p.18. It is not known how it came into the possession of the Silver Studio, but one possibility was that it was given by a wallpaper manufacturer as source material for a similar design.

SD.1549.1979

***165**

Design for a damask tablecloth
31·5 × 54
Gouache on board
c.1895

Probably by Arthur Silver. Note the Art Nouveau whiplash line of the corner motifs, and the fish copied from Japanese prints.

SD.1417.1979

166

Woven silk damask
23 × 37·5
c.1895

This textile has a lush organic design characteristic of Silver Studio productions of the mid 1890s. The colour scheme – deep yellow and mid green on an eau-de-nil ground – was rather old fashioned for this date, and is more typical of aesthetic movement decorative schemes.

ST.26.1979

167

Design for a printed furnishing textile
61 × 52·6
Gouache on cartridge paper
Inscribed *1640*
1895

Probably by Harry Napper. Note the rich colours which were becoming fashionable after the tertiary shades of the 1880s.

SD.1497.1979

***168**

Design for a printed furnishing textile
62·2 × 96·5
Gouache on cartridge paper
Inscribed *1642*
1896

SD.1397.1979

169

Design for a wallpaper
58 × 78·5
Gouache and pencil on cartridge paper
Inscribed *1665*
1896

Aesthetic chintz design of sprays of chrysanthemums

SD.1543.1979

***170**

Design for a wallpaper
66 × 60·5
Gouache on cartridge paper
Inscribed *2144*
1896

Designed by Harry Napper

SD.1207.1979

165

168

172

172

The following designs for book covers (171–87) executed by the Silver Studio for Blackie and Sons over the period 1896–7. The designs by Harry Napper are particularly good and show the influence of Aubrey Beardsley's graphic work.

171

Design for the cover of *Little Ladybird* by L.E.Tiddeman
Gouache on cartridge paper
1896

SD.462.1979

***172**

Trial designs for the cover of *Laugh and Learn – Nursery Lessons and Nursery Games*
Gouache on cartridge paper
Inscribed *No J/Nursery*
1896

SD.461.1979

***173**

Design for the cover of *The Top Brick of the Chimney* by Jennie Chapell
Gouache on cartridge paper
Inscribed *No G/The Top/Brick of/The Chimney/by Jennie/Chapell*
1896

SD.460.1979

***174**

Design for the cover of *Our Little Nan* by Emma Leslie
Gouache on cartridge paper
Inscribed *Our/Little/Nan/by/Emma/Leslie*
1896

SD.458.1979

***175**

Design for the cover of *Brother and Sister* by Elizabeth Lysaght
Gouache on cartridge paper
Inscribed *Brother/&/Sister/by/Elizabeth Lysaght*
1897

Although there is great difficulty in ascribing individual designers to most of these book covers, there can be little doubt that this one is by Harry Napper

SD.459.1979

176

Design for the cover of *The Squire's Grandson* by J.M.Callwell
19 × 28·5
Gouache on cartridge paper with some gold paint
Inscribed *The Squire's Grandson* (twice) *By J.M.Callwell*
1897

SD.1552.1979

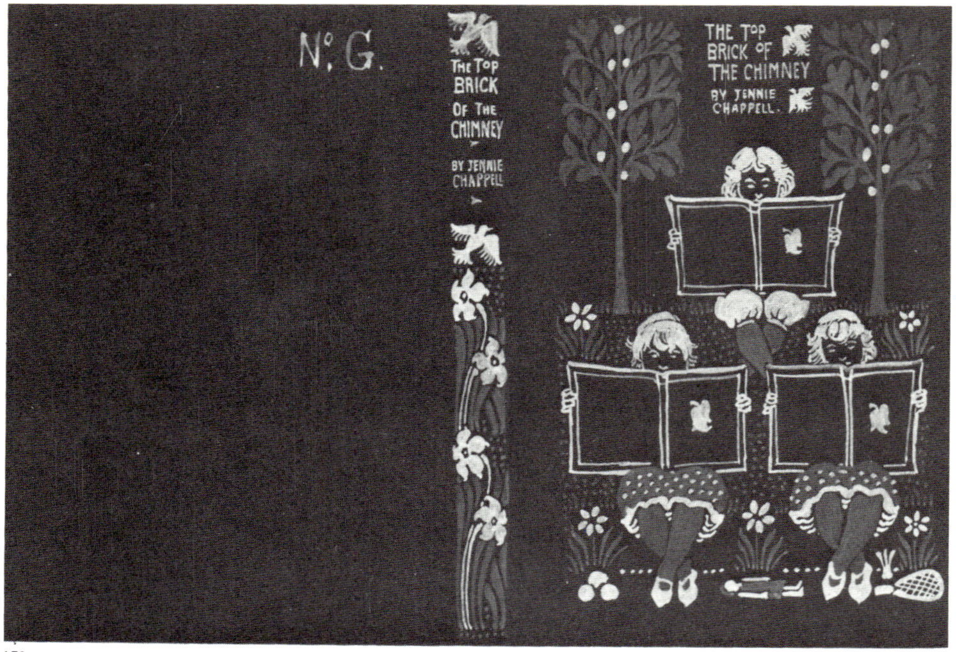
N°. G.
THE TOP BRICK OF THE CHIMNEY
BY JENNIE CHAPPELL
THE TOP BRICK OF THE CHIMNEY
BY JENNIE CHAPPELL.
173

OUR LITTLE NAN
BY EMMA LESLIE
OUR LITTLE NAN
BY
·EMMA·LESLIE·
174

***177**

Design for the cover of *New Light Through Old Windows* by Gregson Gow
Gouache on cartridge paper
Inscribed *New/Light/Through/Old/Windows/by/Gregson/Gow*
1897

SD.457.1979

***178**

Design for the cover of *Girl Neighbours* by Sarah Tyler
Gouache on cartridge paper
Inscribed *Girl/Neighbours/by/Sarah/Tyler*
1897

SD.465.1979

***179**

Design for the cover of *Our Little Nan* by Emma Leslie
Gouache on cartridge paper
Inscribed *Our Little Nan*
1897

SD.466.1979

180

Design for the cover of *The Popular Encyclopedia*
45·5 × 39·3
Pencil and blue crayon on detail paper
Inscribed *The Popular Encyclopedia Vol I*
1897

SD.1158.1979

181

Design for a book cover
46 × 36
Charcoal and red crayon on detail paper
1897

SD.1179.1979

182

Design incorporating Blackie's monogram
35·7 × 26·8
Gouache on detail paper
Inscribed *A2 – C B &S Ltd*
1897

Probably by Harry Napper

SD.1081.1979

183

Design for an end paper for Blackie and Sons Ltd
32·2 × 24·1
Pencil and gouache on detail paper
Inscribed *A2–b*
1897

Probably by Harry Napper

SD.1080.1979

175

177

GIRL NEIGHBOURS
GIRL NEIGH-BOURS
BY SARAH TYTLER
BY
SARAH TYT

178

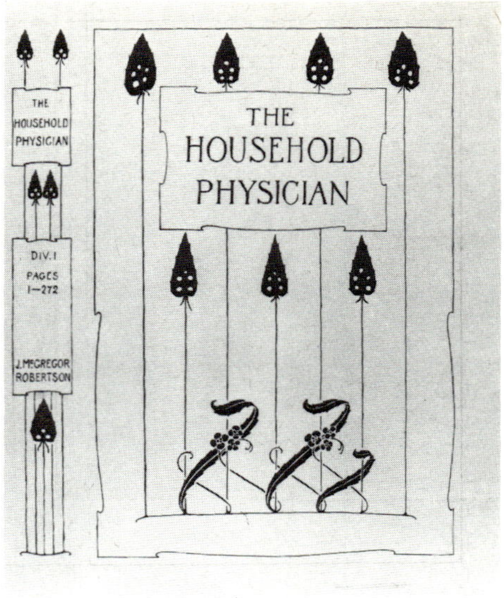
THE HOUSEHOLD PHYSICIAN
DIV. I
PAGES 1—272
J. McGREGOR ROBERTSON
THE
HOUSEHOLD
PHYSICIAN

186

OUR LITTLE NAN
OUR
LITTLE
NAN

179

187

184

Design for Blackie and Sons Ltd
31 × 25
Pencil and gouache on detail paper
Inscribed *A2A*
1897

Delicate, hand-edged Art Nouveau design of rows of chrysanthemums, probably by Harry Napper

SD.1079.1979

185

Design for a book cover
37·6 × 28·5
Charcoal, pencil and red crayon on detail paper
1897

Design of stylized lilies, probably by Harry Napper

SD.1073.1979

***186**

Design for a cover for *The Household Physician* by J. McGregor Robertson
31·4 × 31·2
Black ink on detail paper
Inscribed *The Household Physician/J. McGregor Robertson/Div.1. Pages 1–272*
1897

The design is influenced by Aubrey Beardsley, but the sharp-edged leaves in the lower margin indicate the work of Harry Napper

SD.1089.1979

***187**

Design for the cover of *In the Summer Holidays* by Jennett Humphreys
28·8 × 25·5
Watercolour and gouache on detail paper
Inscribed *In the Summer Holidays/Jennett Humphreys*
1897

Note the influence of C. R. Mackintosh in the drawing of the three girls

SD.1092.1979

***188**

Design for an exhibition label
27·5 × 31·2
Bodycolour on cartridge paper
Inscribed *Designed by J & R Silver*
probably 1897

This design, almost certainly by Harry Napper was probably executed shortly after Arthur Silver's death. The 'J' is for James Silver, Rex Silver's grandfather who had invested money in the Silver Studio on several occasions.

SD.428.1978

***189**

Design for a wallpaper
89·4 × 63
Gouache on cartridge paper
Inscribed *2251*
1897

The severe outlines of this design would suggest the work of Harry Napper

SD.1383.1979

***190**

Wallpaper filling
63 × 91·4
Gouache on cartridge paper
Inscribed *2234*
1897

Designed by Harry Napper

SD.1361.1979

***191**

Design for a wallpaper frieze
63 × 89
Gouache on cartridge paper
Inscribed *2234*
1897

Designed by Harry Napper

SD.1394.1979

***192**

Design for a wallpaper frieze and filling
55·2 × 79·5
Watercolour and charcoal on cartridge paper
Inscribed *2323/Filling/Cornerblock/Self 4h/5 blocks*
1897

There was a growing tendency at the end of the 1890s to use light, clear colours in interior decoration. This was partly to encourage an atmosphere of hygienic lightness and simplicity, and partly as a reaction to the tertiary colours popular in the 1880s and early 1890s. Dutch tiles were also extremely fashionable at this time and used by most important architects in their designs for chimney pieces.

SD.1422.1979

193

Roller-printed cotton
48·9 × 78·7
1897

Design of stylized poppies printed by O'Hanlon from Silver Studio design No.1761

Lent by the Victoria and Albert Museum (Circ.661–1966)

188

190

189

191

192

194

Block-printed silk
71·1 × 61
1897

Design of stylized acanthus leaves and flowers sold to Thomas Wardle in July 1897. Silver Studio design No.1835.

Lent by the Victoria and Albert Museum (Circ.233–1966)

***195**

Design for a woven textile
54·4 × 33
Pencil and gouache on tracing paper
Inscribed *1379*
1898

Two colourways of a Harry Napper design for a woven textile. It was probably for Liberty's, who produced a number of Jaquard woven textiles from Harry Napper's designs at this date.

SD.1286.1979

196

Design for a printed textile
59·7 × 40·5
Charcoal, pastel and gouache on detail paper
Inscribed *04643*
1898

SD.1289.1979

195

Designs for Liberty Metalwork 1898–1910

The authorship of the designs for Liberty metalwork in the Silver Studio Collection has already been the subject of scholarly conjecture by Mrs Shirley Bury.[1] She suggested that some of the designs might well be attributed to Archibald Knox both on stylistic grounds and the fact that some are titled with Isle of Man place names. The only written evidence to concur with this is to be found in an inventory of the Silver Studio Collection taken by Miss Florence Cook (Rex Silver's secretary) in 1933, which refers to 'a parcel of old Knox sketches' in one of the Studio storage rooms. However, there is a quantity of visual and circumstantial evidence to support Mrs Bury's theory.

Rex Silver had personally informed Mrs Bury that he was responsible for much of Liberty's metalwork. This was shortly before his death and he may well have been confused, for even then it was known that a considerable number of people outside the Silver Studio had designed for Liberty metalwork. Before the designs in the collection were discovered the only evidence of Rex's involvement in the Liberty metalwork venture was an illustration of a candlestick, *The Conister*, in *The Studio* magazine of 1900 (Vol. XIX, p.127). In fact this attribution to Rex is meaningless as we now know that Arthur and Rex *never* credited individual studio designers in any public mention of Silver Studio work. Any illustration was invariably ascribed to the head of the Studio. Rex adhered to this principle so rigidly that the editor of *The Studio* magazine refused to give him an entry in *The Designers' Yearbook* of 1909. But of course, in a sense Rex *was* responsible for everything produced by the Studio under his leadership. He suggested, supervised and criticized the designs produced. Winifred Mold, a former designer for the Studio, told the author that although she was usually allowed a free hand in choice of subject matter for a design, if the commission was for a special customer such as Liberty, Rex Silver would take great pains over choosing appropriate source material.

We know from surviving correspondence that Rex was trained by his father to administer the Studio.[2] Rex had admitted to not caring for designing as a career and that he had always wanted to be an artist. He had, however, felt obliged to run the Studio after his father's death in 1896. Although the design staff was managed by Harry Napper until 1898, R.J.Houghton until 1901, and Harry Silver after that, the burden of administration and sale of designs would have rested on Rex's young shoulders. We know from his surviving diaries that this was a more than full-time job. From 1912 the Studio day books list designers' names by the works executed, and from this date until 1963, Rex did not execute one single design. It therefore seems even more unlikely that he had the time to design metalwork for Liberty's over the period 1898–1905, when he would also be learning how to administer the Studio, and indeed being ultimately responsible for the running of it.

Not all the early metalwork designs in the Studio can be attributed to Archibald

Knox. For example a design for a cigarette box of c.1900 seems to be by John Illingworth Kay (see 207). And a very curious feature of all these early metalwork designs is that they were neither given Silver Studio design numbers nor were they photographically recorded. These are the only works by the Silver Studio which were not documented in the usual way. If any of these designs were by Rex, it seems unthinkable that a photographic record was not made.

The metalwork designs produced after 1905 present no such problems. They are numbered, recorded in day books and photographed. And although some owe a debt to the work of Archibald Knox in their use of Celtic motifs, there is little doubt that these are all the work of Rex's brother, Harry Silver. The style and lettering closely relate to designs for textiles, wallpaper and graphic material which are known through information contained in the day books to be by him. Harry Silver's daughter, Mrs Erica Haxworth, has also confirmed that Harry Silver produced designs for Liberty metalwork. She has also suggested that some of the Celtic designs for Liberty's garden pottery produced by Mrs G.F. Watts at the Compton Pottery were also by Harry Silver.

How Archibald Knox actually came to be working for the Silver Studio is also the subject of considerable conjecture. One possibility is that Christopher Dresser introduced him to the Studio, where his son was an apprentice. Liberty's might have recommended Knox to sell his designs through the Studio because the Studio was used to preparing designs to Liberty's requirements. Harry Napper was still design manager of the Studio in October 1898, when the first batch of metalwork designs were sold to Liberty. Napper belonged to the Arts and Crafts Exhibition Society and the Art Workers' Guild and may have met Knox at a meeting of one of these societies. Furthermore, the Silver Studio was very well known in the 1890s and would have been an obvious place to try for part-time or free-lance work. (One must remember that during this early period Archibald Knox was also teaching at Kingston School of Art.)

[1] Mrs Shirley Bury: 'New Light on the Liberty Metalwork Venture' in *The Bulletin of the Decorative Arts Society*, No.1, pp.14–27, 1975

[2] See various letters from Arthur Silver to Rex, 1894–6, in the Silver Studio Collection

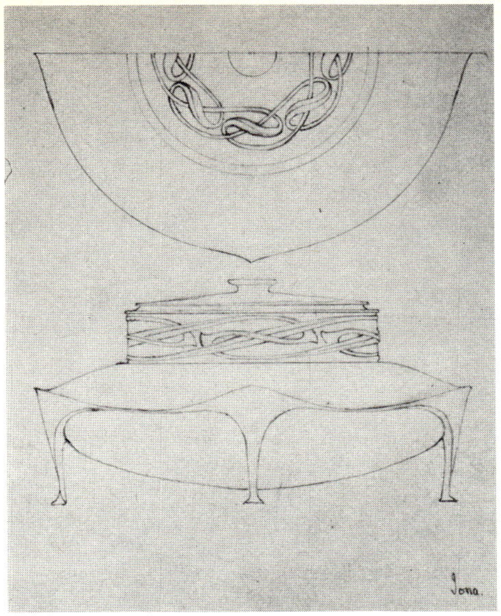

198

The following catalogue entries (197–224) for the period 1898 to 1904 have all been attributed to various designers on stylistic grounds. It is to be hoped that in the future rather more conclusive evidence will come to light.

197

Design for a silver waist clasp
10·3 × 16·5
Pencil on tracing paper
1898

Illustrated in Liberty's *Cymric Silver* Catalogue, pp.92–3
Exhibited at *The Liberty Centenary Exhibition*, Victoria and Albert Museum 1975 (see catalogue p.65, No.123)

Probably by Archibald Knox

SD.2069.1979

***198**

Design for a silver powder bowl, *The Iona*
23 × 21
Pencil on tracing paper
Inscribed *Iona*
1898

Illustrated in Liberty's *Cymric Silver* Catalogue, c.1900, p.37, No.1
Exhibited at *The Liberty Centenary Exhibition*, Victoria and Albert Museum 1975 (see catalogue p.53, D58A)

Probably by Archibald Knox

SD.2077.1979

199

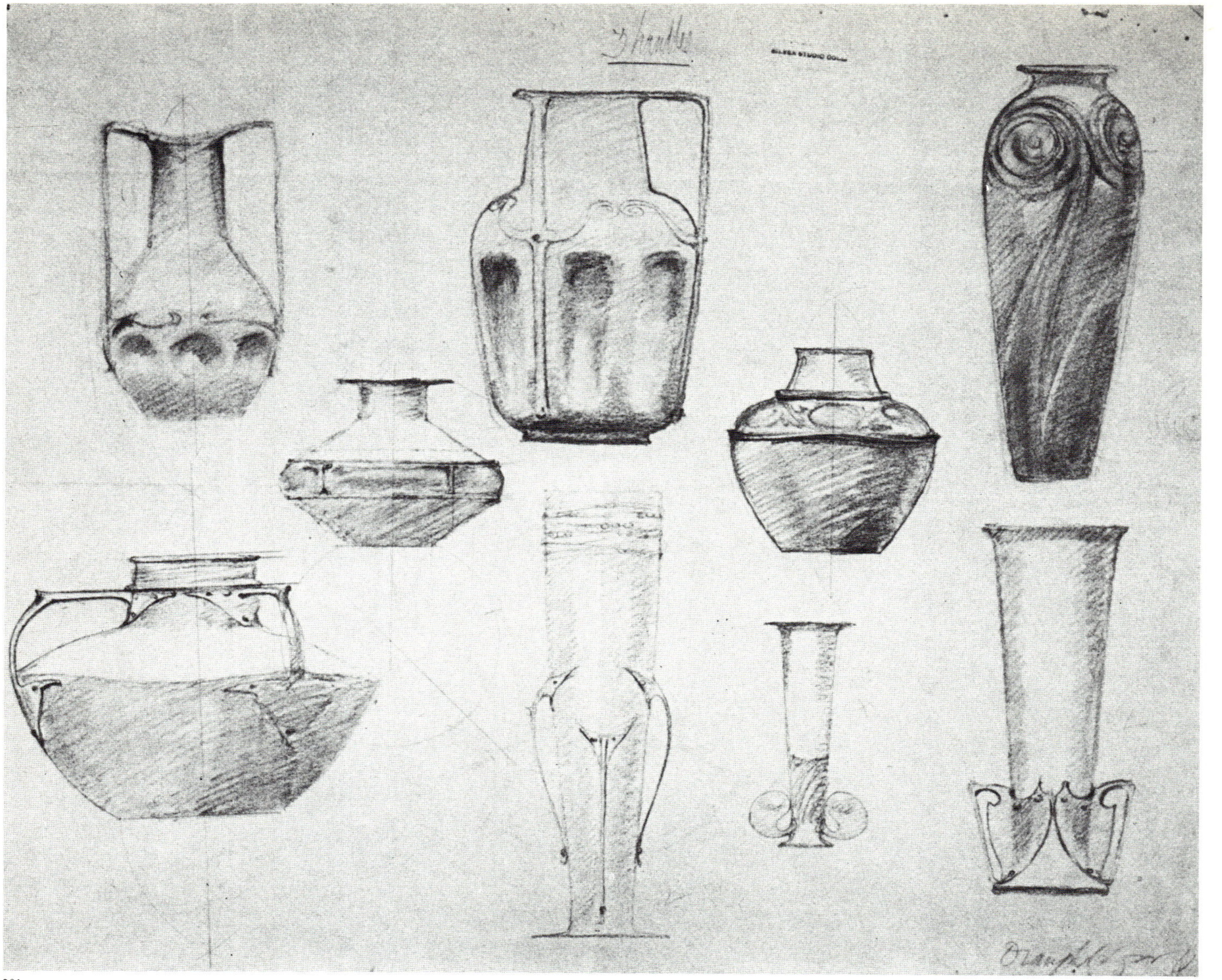

201

***199**

Two designs for silver waist clasps
23·8 × 20·2
Pencil on tracing paper
Inscribed *Flora* and *Clyppan*
1898

The lower design, *Clyppan*, is illustrated in Liberty's *Cymric Silver* Catalogue, c.1900, p.95, No.3

Both designs are probably by Archibald Knox

SD.2059.1979

200

Design for a vase
32·4 × 17·3
Pencil on tracing paper
Inscribed *Cyrus*
1898–9

Illustrated in *The Liberty Centenary Exhibition* Catalogue, Victoria and Albert Museum 1975, p.54, D.60

Harry Silver produced a variation on this design in 1909. The inverted cone shape was one used by Knox in many variations for his designs for vases and jars.

SD.2071.1979

***201**

Sheet of trial designs for vases
46·4 × 55·7
Charcoal and pencil on cartridge paper
Inscribed *Draughts* (*sic*) *for Vases*
1898–9

Illustrations:
Lower centre vase (The *Cyrus*) in *The Liberty Centenary Exhibition* Catalogue 1975, p.54, D60
Lower right-hand vase in *The Liberty Centenary Exhibition* Catalogue 1975, p.64, D112
Upper centre vase illustrated in Liberty's *Cymric Silver* Catalogue, c.1900. p.51, No.1
Upper left-hand vase illustrated in Liberty's *Cymric Silver* Catalogue, c.1900, p.55, No.2
Lower left-hand vase illustrated in Liberty's *Cymric Silver* Catalogue, c.1900, p.57, No.2

Probably by Archibald Knox

SD.1635.1979

202

Design for a silver waist clasp
14 × 21
Pencil on tracing paper
c.1898–9

Illustrated in Liberty's *Cymric Silver* Catalogue, c.1900, p.89, No.1

Probably by Archibald Knox

SD.2070.1979

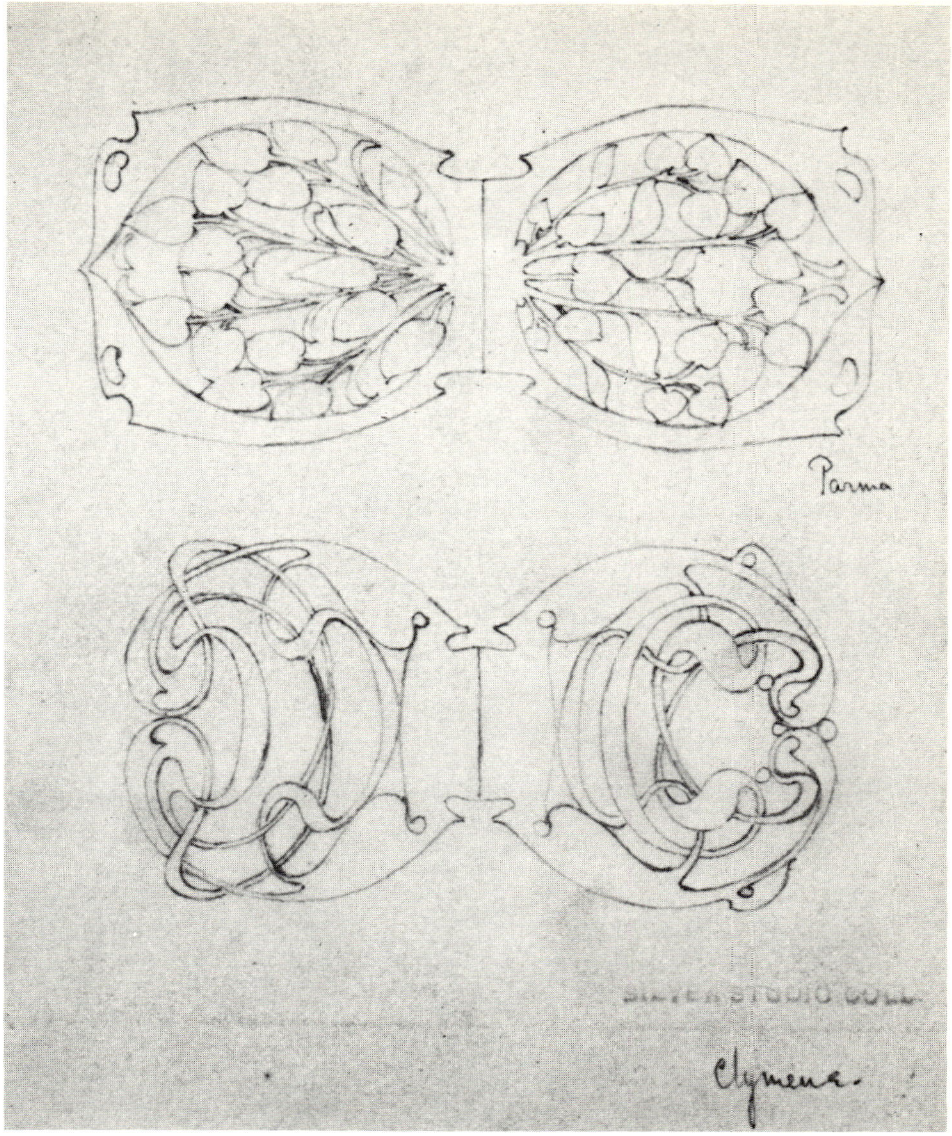

203

***203**

Two sketches for waist clasps
17·2 × 15·6
Pencil on tracing paper
Inscribed *Parma*/*Clymene*
1898–9

The *Clymene* clasp was exhibited at *The Liberty Centenary Exhibition,* Victoria and Albert Museum, 1975, p.66, D129

Illustrated in Liberty's *Cymric Silver* Catalogue, c.1900, pp.94–5, No.3

Probably by Archibald Knox

SD.2068.1979

204

Three trial designs for waist clasps
11 × 25
Pencil on tracing paper
Inscribed *The Phingola/The Aupica/The Fenella/ S2*
1898–9

The *Aupica* is similar to a waist clasp exhibited at *The Liberty Centenary Exhibition*, Victoria and Albert Museum, 1975. See *The Liberty Centenary* Catalogue, 1975, p.66, D130A. The *Fenella* relates to D.134B p.67 in the same catalogue.

Probably by Archibald Knox

SD.2066.1979

***205**

Design for a silver waist clasp
10·5 × 10·1
Pencil on tracing paper
1898–9
Illustrated in Liberty's *Cymric Silver* Catalogue, c.1900, pp.94–5, No.1

Possibly by Archibald Knox, although the stylized flowers suggest the work of Harry Napper

SD.2074.1979

206

Two designs for buckles
20 × 15
Pencil on tracing paper
Inscribed *Cedric* and *Floris*
1898–9

The *Floris* buckle is illustrated in Liberty's *Cymric Silver* Catalogue, c.1900, p.95, No.3

Probably by Archibald Knox

SD.2062.1979

***207**

Design for a cigarette box
51·5 × 73·5
Charcoal, pencil, brown pastel on detail paper
1898–9

This design might be by John Illingworth Kay as the decoration is not dissimilar to the motifs on the gesso casket made by him for his future wife in 1897 (see 17). The design does not appear to have been used.

SD.1676.1979

***208**

Design for a cigarette box
30 × 66·7
Charcoal, pencil, red pastel on detail paper
1898–9

Possibly by John Illingworth Kay. A similar cigarette box was exhibited in *The Liberty Centenary Exhibition*, Victoria and Albert Museum, 1975 (see the catalogue for this exhibition, p.57, No.D75).

SD.1677.1979

209

Design for three silver teaspoons
25 × 21
Pencil on tracing paper
c.1899–1900

The left-hand spoon is illustrated in Liberty's *Cymric Silver* Catalogue, c.1900, p.77, No.1. The right-hand spoon is also illustrated in the same catalogue p.77, No.3. The centre one is illustrated in an adapted form, p.81, No.4, and also in the *Liberty Centenary Exhibition* Catalogue, Victoria and Albert Museum, 1975, p.54, No.D59A as the *Labuan* pattern. All are probably by Archibald Knox.

SD.2080.1979

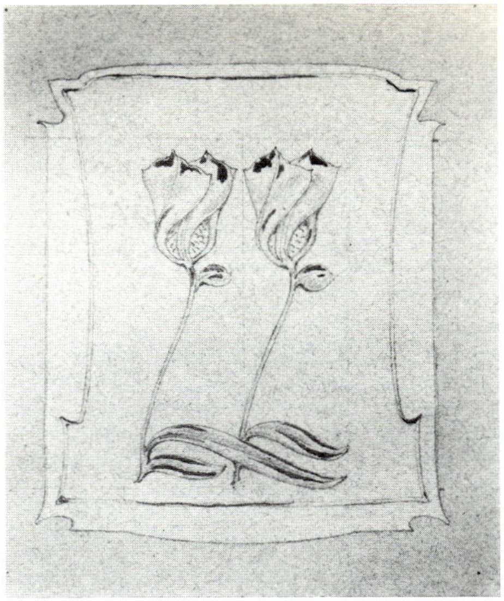

205

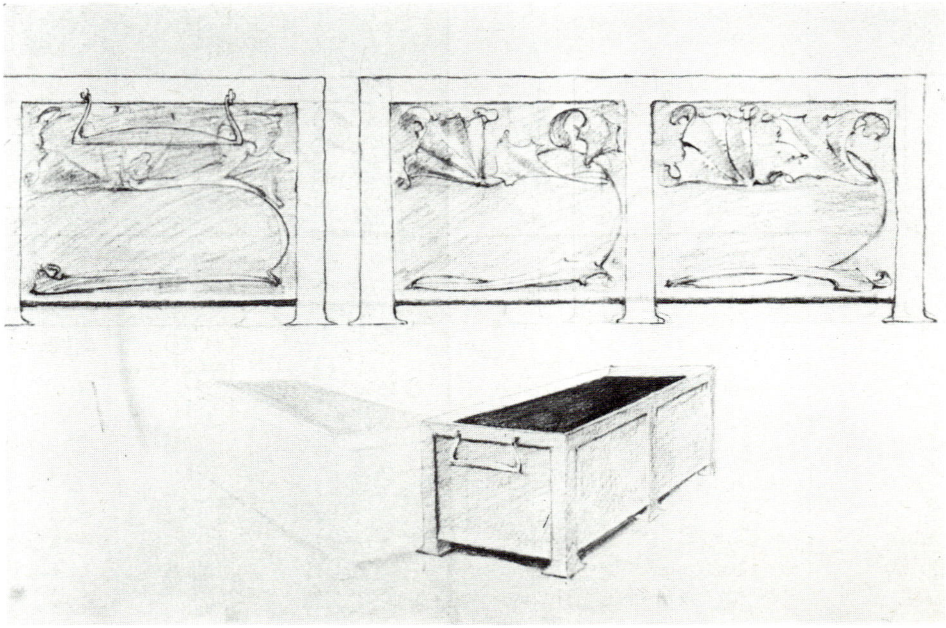

207

210

Design for a silver clock, *The Magnus*
24·2 × 23
Pencil on tracing paper
Inscribed *The Magnus/dial/section at AA*
1899

Exhibited at *The Liberty Centenary Exhibition*, Victoria and Albert Museum, 1975 (see catalogue p.55, D65), where it was attributed to Rex Silver. Note the influence of C.R.Mackintosh in the decoration of the clock façade. Probably by Archibald Knox.

SD.2081.1979

211

Three designs for silver brooches
16·2 × 12·1
Pencil on tracing paper
Inscribed *S.2*
1898–9

The centre design is illustrated in Liberty's *Cymric Silver* Catalogue, c.1900, p.103, No.5. The lower design is also illustrated, p.109, No.5.

Probably by Archibald Knox

SD.2078.1979

212

Design for a powder puff bowl and lid, *The Memphis*
26·3 × 18
Inscribed *Memphis/Top/Front*
1898

Illustrated in Liberty's *Cymric Silver* Catalogue, c.1900, pp.42–3, No.2. Amongst the first metalwork designs to be sold to Liberty in October 1898 were two designs for powder bowls.

Probably by Archibald Knox

SD.2076.1979

213

Design for a silver flower bowl
29 × 24
Pencil on tracing paper
1899

Illustrated in Liberty's *Cymric Silver* Catalogue, c.1900, pp.56–7, No.2

Probably by Archibald Knox

SD.2075.1979

214

A sheet of trial designs for silver vases
50 × 69·6
Pencil and charcoal on cartridge paper
Inscribed in red pencil *Draughts* (*sic*) *for Vases*
1899

The following were illustrated in Liberty's *Cymric Silver* Catalogue of c.1900: Lower right-hand vase p.55, No.1, Middle left-hand vase (with scroll top legs) p.49, No.3, Middle right-hand vase p.43, No.2

Probably by Archibald Knox

SD.1618.1979

215

Two designs for silver clocks
41·5 × 30·5
Pencil on tracing paper
Inscribed *The Sigurd* and inscribed on dial *Tempis Fugit*, *The Olaf* and inscribed on dial *Festina Lente*
1899–1900

The Olaf was illustrated in Liberty's *Cymric Silver* Catalogue, c.1900, p.56, No.1

Probably by Archibald Knox

SD.2065.1979

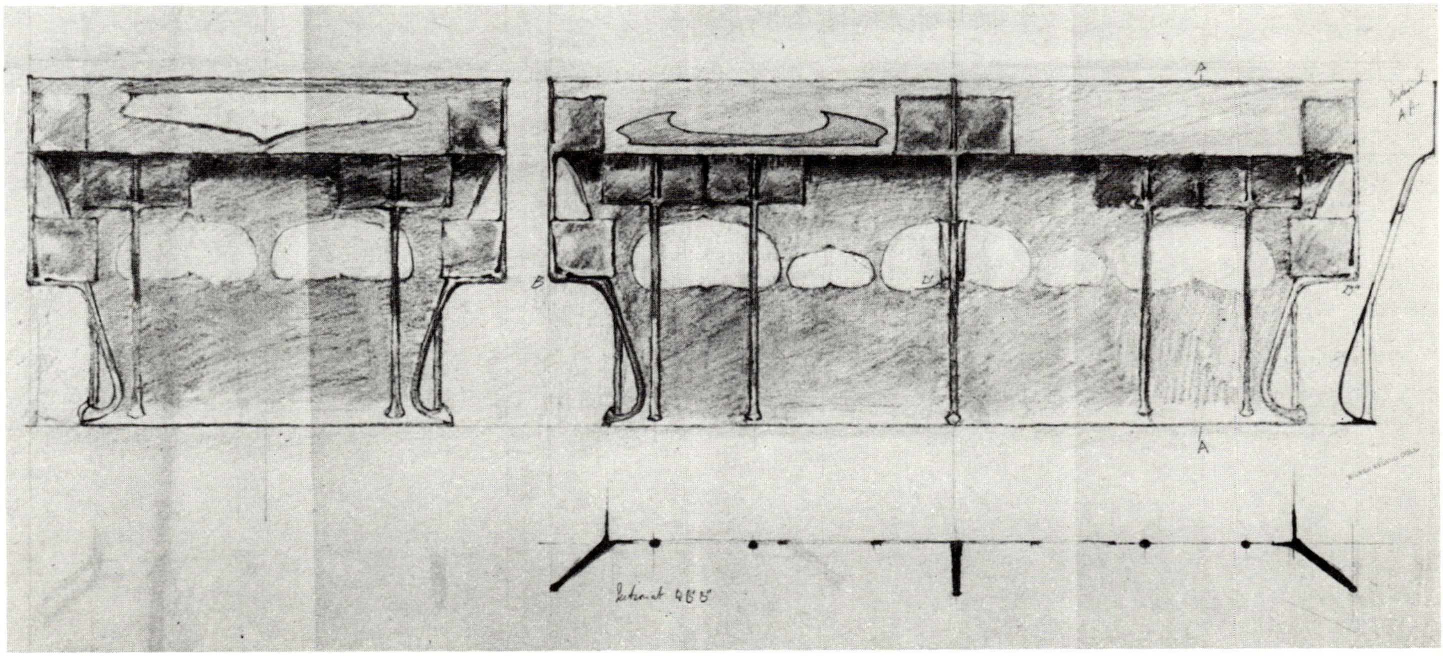

208

216
Two designs for silver spoons
28 x 21
Pencil on tracing paper
Inscribed *The Neeba/S.3/The Neb*
c.1899–1900

The right-hand spoon is illustrated in Liberty's *Cymric Silver* Catalogue, c.1900, p.75, No.1

Probably by Archibald Knox

SD.2079.1979

217
Design for a silver waist clasp
14·2 x 20
Pencil on tracing paper
c.1900

In *The Liberty Centenary Exhibition* at the Victoria and Albert Museum, 1975, this clasp was attributed to A.C.Craythorn (p.68, D.138)

Probably by Archibald Knox

SD.2067.1979

218
Design for a silver bag mount
45 x 28
Pencil on tracing paper
Inscribed *Rozelan*
c.1900

Illustrated in Liberty's *Cymric Silver* Catalogue, c.1900, p.99, No.1

Probably by Archibald Knox

SD.2058.1979

219
Two sketches of a design for a silver match box
each 5·3 x 10
Pencil and watercolour on cartridge paper
Inscribed *Vesta*
c.1900

Note the influence of C.R.Mackintosh on the stylized plant forms in the decoration of these designs

SD.2073.1979

220
Design for a silver photograph frame
39·7 x 32·3
Pencil, crayon and wash on detail paper
Inscribed *The Rhaa*
c.1900

The stylized leaves, inset enamel and Celtic scroll work all indicate the work of Archibald Knox

SD.2072.1979

223

221

Design for a silver photograph frame
39·5 × 27·5
Pencil and crayon on detail paper
Inscribed *The Rhenny*
c.1900

Probably by Archibald Knox

SD.2063.1979

222

Design for a photograph frame
31 × 25·5
Pencil on detail paper
Inscribed *Arrosey*
c.1900

Designed by Archibald Knox

SD.2060.1979

***223**

Design for a pewter dish or tray
39 × 31·8
Pencil on tracing paper
Inscribed *Bollellin*
c.1903

Illustrated in Liberty Catalogue No.83, for 1903, p.39, No.1, *Liberty Centenary Exhibition* Catalogue, 1975, p.75, No.D185, where it is attributed to Archibald Knox

Probably by Archibald Knox

SD.2064.1979

***224**

Design for a pewter bowl
52 × 55
Pencil on tracing paper
Inscribed *Godfred* and with working notes in Harry Silver's hand
1903–4

Tracing by Harry Silver, probably from an original design by Archibald Knox. Circular bowl with design of swirling tendrils and stylized leaves. Design was finally used without handles. (See 246.)

SD.2108.1979

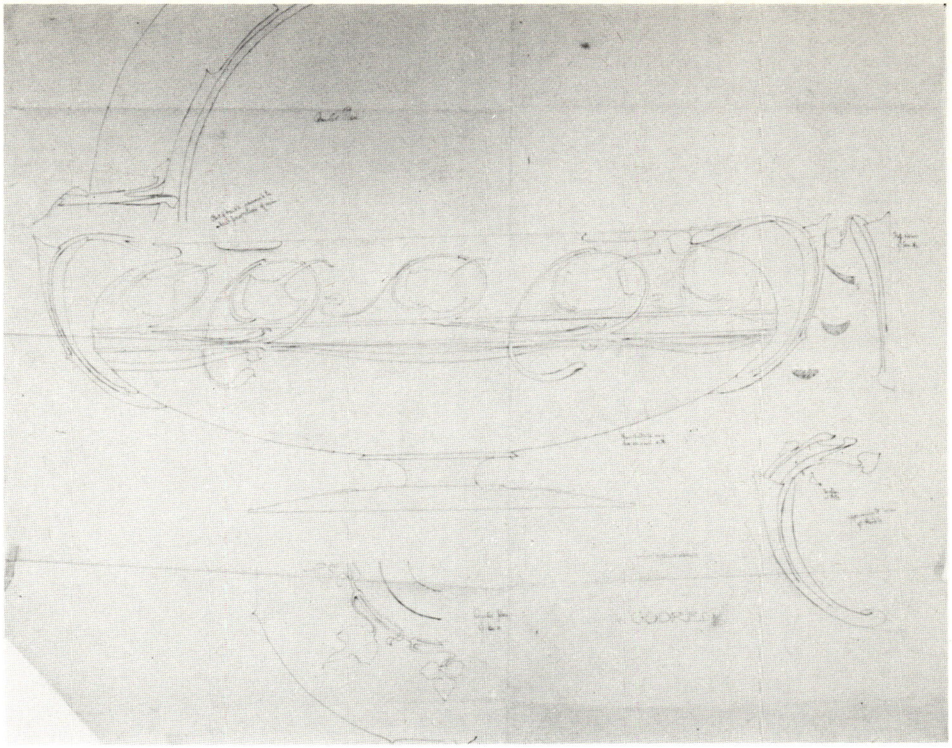

224

The following four designs (225–8) have been attributed to Archibald Knox on stylistic grounds. They are for damasks, but the motifs relate to Knox's metalwork.

225

Design intended for damask but used for a lace curtain
45·5 × 42
Pencil on tracing paper
Inscribed *03393/A/60"/used as lace curtain*
1901

SD.2030.1979

226

Design for a damask
43·5 × 48
Pencil on detail paper
Inscribed *02736/N.S./A*
1900

SD.2031.1979

227

Design for a damask
26·5 × 26
Pencil on detail paper
Inscribed *Alternative/filling to/No 02736 (N.S.)*
1900

SD.2032.1979

228

Design for a damask
41 × 35
Pencil on detail paper
Inscribed *02727 N.S.*
1900

SD.2033.1979

The following metalwork designs (229–49b) are by Harry Silver. Unlike the Knox designs (which influenced Harry's work) these are nearly all given Silver Studio design numbers; and those executed after 1906 are recorded in the relevant day book, and photographic record. Some of these designs reflect the influence of Knox, in the use of Celtic ornament, and others reflect the growing interest in neo-eighteenth-century decoration, and the small geometric patterns which characterised British Art Nouveau in the early 1900s.

229

Two designs for waist clasps
26 × 28·5
Pencil and watercolour on green cartridge paper
c.1904

These two designs may be by Harry Silver, as they are altered versions of Knox's *Parma* and *Clymene* clasps (see 203). We know from the Studio day books that Liberty sent metalwork designs to the Silver Studio for alteration, and two similar designs on green cartridge paper are numbered in Harry Silver's hand, and datable at 1904 from the design number. (See 230)

SD.1672

230

Two designs for waist clasps
37·5 × 21·5
Pencil and watercolour on green cartridge paper
Inscribed *05023*
1904

By Harry Silver, but strongly influenced by Knox

SD.1670.1979

231

Design for a silver tray
27·7 × 29·5
Pencil and watercolour on green cartridge paper
Inscribed *05025*
1904

Probably by Harry Silver, but influenced by Archibald Knox

SD.1673.1979

232

Two designs for an ice and coffee spoon
46·3 × 33·3
Pencil on detail paper
Inscribed in pencil *Ice* and *Coffee*
1909

These designs by Harry Silver were part of a large order sold to Liberty on 26 April 1909. (Silver Studio design No.06555)

SD.1629.1979

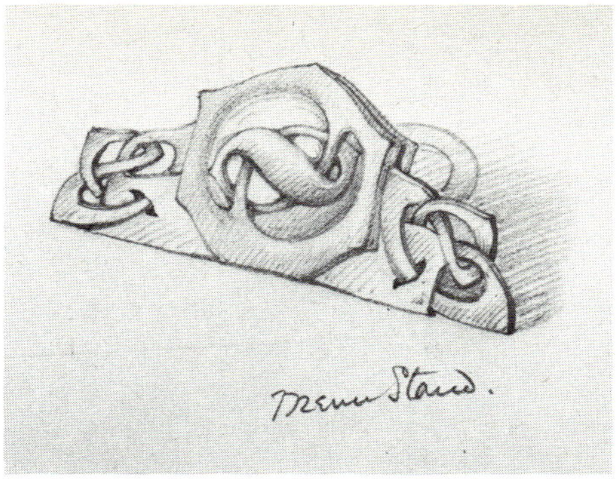

234

233

Design for a fork and two knives
45·5 × 33
Pencil on detail paper
Inscribed *Fork for Fruit or Fish/Fruit knife/Fish knife*
1909

By Harry Silver

SD.1634.1979

***234**

Design for a silver menu stand
27 × 29·5
Pencil on detail paper
Inscribed (in Rex Silver's hand) *Menu Stand*
1909

By Harry Silver

SD.2061.1979

235

Sketch for a silver clock
42·5 × 33·7
Inscribed (in Harry Silver's hand) *5" High/Side View/06831*
1910

This design was sold to Liberty on 10 May 1910, for £3.13s.6d. (See 224)

SD.1642.1979

236

A selection of designs for the decoration of silver christening sets
45·7 × 39·5
Pencil on detail paper
Inscribed *06836/06838/06835/06837* and working notes
1910

The Silver Studio ultimately sold four designs for silver christening sets to Liberty in 1910

SD.1663.1979

237

Design for a christening set
53·6 × 40
Pencil on detail paper
Inscribed *06838/used with alterations*
1910

By Harry Silver with a motif of stylized briar roses

SD.1667.1979

238

Design for a silver christening set
44·7 × 34·2
Pencil and watercolour on detail paper
Inscribed *06835*
1910

The use of check borders in enamel probably derives from the work of C. R. Mackintosh – this type of geometrical decoration was extremely influential in Austria and France

SD.1646.1979

239

Pair of candlesticks
Height 24·2
Stamped *L & C* and with Birmingham Hallmark for 1906
1906

Exhibited at *The Liberty Centenary Exhibition*, Victoria and Albert Museum 1975, No.D64
These candlesticks were illustrated in *The Studio*, Vol. XIX, p.127, and attributed to Rex Silver. In fact, it is likely that these were from a design by Archibald Knox whilst working at the Silver Studio, but, like all designs produced by the Studio, were credited to the Studio's director.

Lent by the Victoria and Albert Museum (Circ.165&a.1959)

240

Set of six silver teaspoons
Length: 11
Inscribed One spoon stamped *Cymric*, other five are stamped *L & Co*
1903

Illustrated in Liberty Catalogue for 1899, p.44, No.4
Exhibited at *The Liberty Centenary Exhibition*, Victoria and Albert Museum, 1975, No.D.61

From a design of 1899, probably by Archibald Knox. Stems of spoons decorated with simple stylized leaves set on green enamel ground. The original design is in the Silver Studio Collection.

Lent by the Victoria and Albert Museum (. . . . .)

241

Casket
Length 21·6
Stamped *L & Co.* and with Birmingham Hallmark for 1903
1903

Exhibited at *The Liberty Centenary Exhibition*, Victoria and Albert Museum, 1975, No.D101

The extremely fine quality of the interlace decoration of this casket would suggest that this is the work of Archibald Knox. This piece belonged to A.L.Liberty and was subsequently acquired by Knox's pupil Mrs Denise Wren, as a Knox piece.

Lent by the Victoria and Albert Museum (M15–1970)

242

Dressing table set of pin tray, button hook, glove tongues and shoe horn
Stamped with Birmingham Hallmark for 1904 and *L & Co.*
1904

Silver, set with turquoises. The small Celtic motifs would suggest that this is the work of Harry Silver.

Lent by the Victoria and Albert Museum (M315–318–1979)

243

Christening set in fitted case
Length of spoon 15
Spoon and fork stamped with Birmingham Hallmark for 1912 and *5790*
Napkin ring stamped *L & Co* and engraved *Gay*

Given to Harry Silver's daughter, Gay, as a christening present. Designed by Harry B.Silver, original design in the Silver Studio Collection.

Lent by Mrs Herman Silver

244

Silver clock
15 × 9.7
Inscribed, on base, *L & Co* and stamped *5789*
1911

From Silver Studio design No.06831. By Harry Silver.

Lent by Mr and Mrs William Haxworth

245

Pewter bowl
Width 29·2
Inscribed *Rd/4/420/English Pewter/Made by Liberty & Co/0229*

Illustrated in Liberty's Catalogue No.107, 1905–6, p.79
1903

Pewter bowl with two handles which extend beneath the bowl to form the feet. Decorated with a design of stylized flowers which could be either by Archibald Knox or Harry Silver.

Lent by the Victoria and Albert Museum (Circ.275–1961)

246

Pewter flower bowl
Diameter 37·5
Inscribed *Tudoric/06*
Illustrated in Liberty's *Yule Tide Gifts* Catalogue for 1904, p.38, No.4
c.1904

Bowl decorated with design of stylized leaves and swirling tendrils. Probably by Archibald Knox (see 224).

Lent by the Victoria and Albert Museum (Circ.910–1967)

247

Pewter crumb scoop
8·3 × 25
c.1905

Illustrated in Liberty's *Yule Tide Gifts* Catalogue for 1907

Design registered on 1 July, 1905. Decorated with motifs of stylized leaves and with Celtic scrollwork. Possibly by Harry Silver.

Lent by the Victoria and Albert Museum (Circ.921–1967)

251

248

Pewter ink stand
4 × 22
Inscribed, on base, *English Pewter/Made by/ Liberty & Co/0404*
c.1905

Decorated with a design of stylized briar leaves and scroll work – motifs used by both Archibald Knox and Harry Silver. The slight coarseness of detail might possibly indicate that this design is by Harry.

Lent by Peter Haxworth, Esq.

249(a)

Pewter butter dish
4·7 × 17·3
Inscribed on base *0163*
c.1905

Design of stylized leaves shows the influence of Archibald Knox, but this piece is almost certainly by Harry Silver

Lent by Mr and Mrs William Haxworth

249(b)

Liberty & Co Catalogue *Yule Tide Gifts*
18·5 × 24·5
1901
See pp.52–3 for illustrations of clasps and buckles executed from designs supplied by the Silver Studio

P.52 No.1 Waist clasp probably by Harry Napper
P.53 No.5 Buckle by Archibald Knox

SE.463.1979

250 colour plate IV,b

Woven silk and cotton doublecloth
29 × 34
1898

From Silver Studio design No.11800(b) sold to Leborgne in 1898. Design of stylized briar roses and whiplash Art Nouveau stripe. Golden yellow, pale blue, green and red on cream ground. This is typical of the richly coloured Art Nouveau designs sold to French textile manufacturers in the late 1890s.

ST.40.1979

***251**

Design for a wallpaper
48 × 56·3
Gouache on cartridge paper
Inscribed *2328*
1898

Designed by Harry Napper. Note the influence of Aubrey Beardsley in this design.

SD.2056.1979

253

256

252
Design for a printed textile
60·6 × 45·4
Gouache on cartridge paper
Inscribed *4*
1898

This design illustrates the Silver Studio's use of rich, dark colours at this period

SD.2050.1979

***253**
Design for a printed textile
74·5 × 60
Gouache on cartridge paper
Inscribed *1960*
1898

Designed by Harry Napper

SD.2043.1979

254
Design for a wallpaper
40·5 × 49
Gouache on cartridge paper
Inscribed *5*
1898

Designed by Harry Napper

SD.2042.1979

255
Roller-printed cotton
48·3 × 78·7
1898

From a design of stylized poppies by Harry Napper, and printed by Stonard. Silver Studio design No.1922.

Lent by the Victoria and Albert Museum (Circ.662.1966)

***256**
Wallpaper
29 × 50·8
1898

'Sanitary' machine-printed wallpaper with design of stylized tulips on imitation tile ground. This is an example of a 'Sanitary' wallpaper – viz. wallpaper printed by engraved copper rollers to produce a smooth surface which could be varnished and so rendered washable.

SW.62.1976

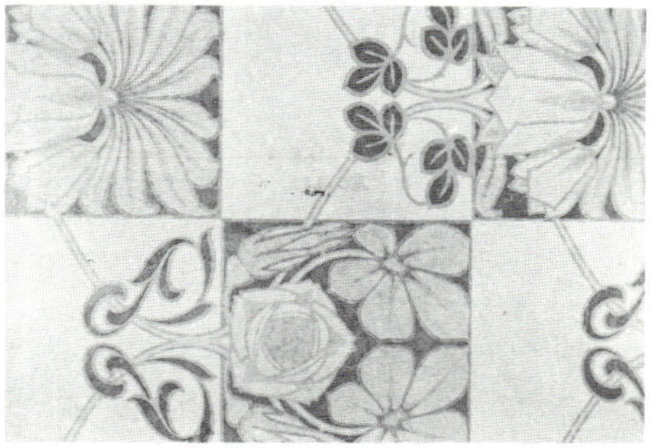
257

***257**
Wallpaper
37 × 25·5
Varnished and distemper on paper
Inscribed, *verso, Sanitary/9411/3s 6d per piece*
1898–9

From Silver Studio design No.2503. A 'Sanitary' wallpaper, probably manufactured by Allan Cockshutt for Rottmann and Co., from a design by Harry Napper.

SW.74.1976

259

258
Design for a printed furnishing textile
56·8 × 61·6
Gouache on cartridge paper
Inscribed *No.2026*
1899

SD.2054.1979

***259**
Design for a wallpaper
51 × 40
Body-colour on cartridge paper
Inscribed *2682*
1899

This design is one of the earliest to show the increasing formality of Art Nouveau designs which occurred in the early 1900s

SD.427.1979

***260**
Design for a wallpaper
65·5 × 52·4
Gouache on green sugar paper
Inscribed *2608*
1899

Design adapted from a Voysey wallpaper based on a bird holding a stylized flower, in two colours

SD.2052.1979

260

261
Design for a wallpaper
65·5 × 48
Gouache on cartridge paper
Inscribed *2232*
1899

By Harry Napper

SD.2053.1979

262
Woven silk and cotton doublecloth
76·2 × 63·5
1899

From Silver Studio design No.12058. The pronounced Art Nouveau whiplash motif of the design, and the elongated flowers suggest that this is possibly the work of Archibald Knox. The economy and extreme stylisation of the design is not dissimilar to motifs used on his designs for Liberty metalwork.

Lent by the Victoria and Albert Museum (Circ.288.1966)

263
Woven cotton
68 × 39·4
1899

From Silver Studio design No.12136, probably by Harry Napper, of stylized flowers and leaves

Lent by the Victoria and Albert Museum (Circ.250.1966)

264
Woven wool tapesty
65·4 × 35·6
1899

Design of acanthus and flowers, probably by Harry Napper and from Silver Studio design No.12084

Lent by the Victoria and Albert Museum (Circ.254.1966)

***265**
Design for a wallpaper
64 × 71
Gouache on cartridge paper
Inscribed *No. 2126*
1899

Design of stylized buttercups, probably by John Illingworth Kay

SD.2046.1979

265

266

***266**
Design for a wallpaper
69·5 × 62
Gouache on cartridge paper
Inscribed *2471*
1899–1900

Inspired by William Morris wallpapers such as the *St James* of 1881, but in gentler colours

SD.2045.1979

***267**
Christmas card
Inscribed *With/Best Wishes/for Xmas/and the New Year/1899/R.S.*
1899

By Rex Silver

SE.487.1979

268
Design for a Liberty share certificate
34 × 50
Pencil and ink on detail paper
Inscribed *Liberty and Co. Limited, Preference Stock Certificate*
1899

The two Art Nouveau motifs included in this design suggest the work of Harry Napper

SD.1117.1979

269
Design for a wallpaper frieze
40·2 × 70·3
Gouache, crayon and charcoal on detail paper
Inscribed *04344*
c.1900

This design of stylized flowers and acanthus scrolls was altered and sold as a wallpaper frieze (see 270). The design was probably by Harry Silver.

SD.2111.1980

***270**
27·5 × 51·5
c.1900

'Sanitary' machine-printed wallpaper frieze with design of stylized roses and acanthus leaves from Silver Studio design No.2606. A trial design for this frieze is also included in this exhibition (see 269).

SW.70.1976

271
Trade card for Alexander Rottmann & Co.
13 × 18
c.1900

Designed by Harry Napper, who frequently supplied wallpaper and stencil designs to Rottmann after leaving the Silver Studio in 1898

SE.477.1979

272
Wool tapestry
45 × 30·5
c.1900

Manufactured by Vanoutyre et Cie from a design by Harry Silver of heart-shaped leaves arranged in vertical stripes, in green, pale blue, pale pink on ochre ground

ST.52.1979

267

270

273

304

275

***273**

Trade card for Essex Wallpapers
12 × 17
Inscribed *Essex and Company's Westminster Wall/ Papers 114–116 Victoria/Street Westminster/and at Essex Mills/Battersea London*
c.1900

The Silver Studio based a number of designs for graphic work on this design by Voysey (see 274)

SE.503.1979

274

Christmas card
14 × 16
Distemper on hand-made paper
Inscribed *With best/wishes for/Xmas/and the/New Year*
c.1900

A very strong Voysey influence is apparent in this design, both in its formal qualities and, of course, the use of stylized birds

SE.489.1979

***275**

Christmas card
Inscribed *With Best/Wishes for Xmas &/The New Year*
c.1900

Probably by Harry Silver, and reflects his admiration for Archibald Knox and C.F.A. Voysey

SE.507.1979

276

Silk tissue
68 × 64
c.1900

Manufacturd by Leborgne from a design by Harry Napper of vertical stripes, some containing motifs of stylized flowers in brilliant colours on pale grey ground, others containing stylized flowers in gold on olive or light green grounds

ST.51.1979

***277**

Design for a printed textile
97 × 71·5
Pastel on detail paper
Inscribed *475ns*
c.1900

Design of stylized trees and leaves with deer and pheasants

SD.2005.1979

***278**

Design for a printed furnishing textile
77 × 55
Gouache, charcoal and crayon on detail paper
Inscribed *657/n.s/6 colours*
c.1900
Simple, Voysey-influenced design of deer and stylized trees. The trial colour scheme in the lower left-hand corner was a device used by the Silver Studio to give a prospective customer some idea of how the design would look when finished.

SD.2004.1979

279

Machine-printed wallpaper
29·4 × 50·7
c.1900

An example of a 'Sanitary' wallpaper produced by Harry Napper for Rottmann & Co.

SW.62.1976

277

278

281

280

Wallpaper
58·5 × 61
Distemper on paper
c.1900

Based on Silver Studio design No.2617

SW.67.1976

***281**

Design for a printed textile
54·2 × 41·2
Pastel on tracing paper
Inscribed *04190*
c.1900

Green and orange Art Nouveau design of stylized buttercups, in the style of Harry Napper

SD.1500.1979

282

Woven silk damask
38 × 31
c.1900

This damask was produced from Silver Studio design No.12728 and shows two fashionable elements – French Rococo design and Japanese art. Damask was still very fashionable for smart town houses and grand hotels, where the emphasis was on opulence, rather than design-consciousness.

ST.25.1979

***283(a)**

Design for a wallpaper
41·5 × 31
Charcoal, crayon, gouache on detail paper
Inscribed *No.03338*
c.1900

SD.1490.1979

***283(b)**

Design for a wallpaper
35·8 × 26
Watercolour on tracing paper
Inscribed *03899E*
c.1900

This design of stylized flowering bushes on a plain ground is derived from designs by C.F.A.Voysey, such as his *Squire's Garden* wallpaper of 1898

SD.429.1978

283(a)

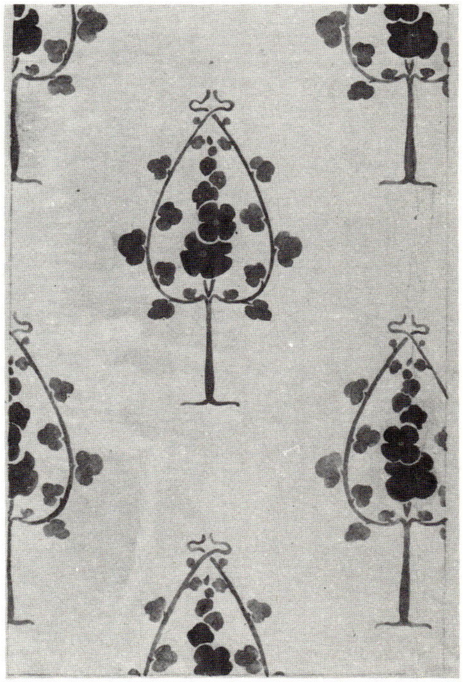

283(b)

285

286

284 colour plate IV,a

Woven silk and cotton cloth
60 × 30
c.1900

This was produced from Silver Studio design No.12264 by John Illingworth Kay, and is an excellent example of his Art Nouveau style

ST.12.1979

***285**

Design for a wallpaper
46 × 32·5
Gouache on cartridge paper
Inscribed *32612*
c.1900–5

This is a design for a cheap wallpaper meant to imitate a woven textile. Note the development of tight, formal qualities in English Art Nouveau at this date.

SD.432.1978

***286**

Design for a woven textile
45·5 × 43·8
Pencil and gouache on tracing paper
Inscribed 2046.n.s.
c.1900

Probably by John Illingworth Kay for Liberty & Co.

SD.1284.1979

287

Design for a book plate (in a sketch book)
20·8 × 14·9
Pencil on detail paper
Inscribed *Ex Libris/Reginald/Silver/Date*
c.1900–5

Design based on stylized briar roses with a border of tulips

SE.603.1979

288

Catalogue for *An Officer's Ideal Quarters*
22 × 15
1901

Produced by Messrs Norman and Stacey Ltd, a well-known firm of furnishers and interior decorators, containing furniture, metalwork, chimney pieces, light fittings and wallpapers designed by Harry Napper. (For further information on this venture of Napper's, see catalogue introduction.)

SE.480.1979

***289**

Design for a Christmas card
46 × 65·7
India ink and white lead on cartridge paper
Inscribed *Good Fortune/With Best Wishes/For Xmas and the New Year/1901 and 1902*
1901

Probably designed by Harry Silver

SD.1560.1979

290

Design for a Christmas card
45 × 37
Pencil on tracing paper
Inscribed *Xmas Card 1901*
1901

SD.1151.1979

291

Design for a wallpaper frieze
61·5 × 89
Pastel on detail paper
Inscribed *03329*
1902

Voysey-inspired design of stylized trees, birds and deer on a light ground

SD.1424.1979

292

Two pages of design motifs in a sketch book
11·5 × 36·5
Pencil on cartridge paper
Inscribed *Ideas*
1903–4

By Harry Silver. Some of the designs in this sketch book are dated 1903, others, 1904. Note Harry's very delicate, Voysey-ish style, with great emphasis on formality and stylisation.

Lent by Mr and Mrs William Haxworth

293 colour plate III,c

Design for a printed textile
53·5 × 44·7
Watercolour and pencil on detail paper
Inscribed *04821*
1903

Simple Arts and Crafts design of peacocks and stylized trees on light ground, probably by Harry Silver

SD.1227.1979

289

294

***294**

Design for a cushion cover
72 × 71
Watercolour, pencil on tracing paper
Inscribed *04894*
1903

By Harry Silver, and showing the influence of Archibald Knox in the use of Celtic ornament

SD.2082.1979

295

Woven silk
22·5 × 11·5
1903

Woven silk tissue from Silver Studio design No.13180. Label, *verso*, inscribed *No.101/ Norfolk*.

ST.16.1979

296

Block-printed cotton
11 × 49·5
1903

This sample was printed from Silver Studio design No.32216 and shows the tendency to simplicity and formality which characterised later English Art Nouveau designs

ST.27.1979

***297**

Design for a calendar
48 × 34·3
Pencil and watercolour on detail paper
Inscribed *The 1904 Calendar/Jan:/03803B*
1903

The Silver Studio produced a number of designs based on heraldic motifs in the period 1900–10. So did other designers, including Voysey. Note the use of Celtic ornament on the framework of the design.

SD.1182.1979

298

Watercolour and charcoal sketches for a design for a cushion cover
73 × 72·2 and 19·5 × 19·5
Inscribed in pencil *04417*
1903

SD.1435.1979

***299**

Design for a printed furnishing textile
65·5 × 73
Crayon on detail paper
Inscribed *05067n.s.*
1904

Doubtless influenced by Voysey's heraldic designs (the Silver Studio Collection contains a Voysey wallpaper for the Coronation of Edward VII which is very similar to this design)

SD.2003.1979

297

299

300

***300**

Design for a wallpaper
61·5 × 44·5
Gouache on cartridge paper
Inscribed *2685/G/S*
1904

Simple late Art Nouveau design for a cheap two-colour wallpaper

SD.1498.1979

***301**

Design for a printed furnishing textile
38·5 × 25·1
Watercolour on cartridge paper
Inscribed in pencil *05891*
1904

This is one of the first period designs produced by the Silver Studio since 1895, and is based on Jacobean embroidery

SD.1493.1979

***302**

Design for a printed textile
44·5 × 42·7
Watercolour on tracing paper
Inscribed in pencil *04867*
1904

Late Art Nouveau design of stylized waterlilies on light ground

SD.1287.1979

***303**

Design for a wallpaper border
53·5 × 69·5
Watercolour and charcoal on detail paper
Inscribed *G/04101*
1904

Simple, stylized design based on Voysey's work. Note the gradation of colours to emulate stencilling.

SD.2007.1979

301

302

303

***304**

Christmas card
13·5 × 7·5
Inscribed *Greetings/and Good/wishes/from all at/ 84 Brook/Green W./1904–5/From I. and R.Silver*
1904

The *I. and R.Silver* refers to Isabelle (Rex's mother) and Rex Silver. The design is very much an imitation of Voysey's work and may possibly have been by Harry Silver.

SE.488.1979

***305**

Design for a cushion square
73·5 × 71
Pencil and crayon on detail paper
Inscribed *04973*
1904

Design of flat, stylized plants, rabbits and deer, probably by Harry Silver

SD.2083.1979

The following designs (306–8) were executed by Harry Silver for Blackie and Sons Ltd, in 1904

306

Design for a cover for *Dick Chester* by G.I.Witham
26 × 25
Pencil and gouache on detail paper
Inscribed *Dick Chester* (twice)/*By G I Witham* (twice)/*Blackie & Sons Limited/04496/S.7*
1904

Influenced by the graphic work of the Beggarstaff brothers

SD.1071.1979

307

Design for a book cover for *Adventures in Field and Flood*
32 × 29·7
Gouache and pencil on detail paper
Inscribed *Adventures in Field and Flood* (twice), *verso, P/05141/S.12*
1904

SD.1103.1979

308

Design for a book cover for *The Deer Slayer* by J.Fennimore Cooper
343 × 32·4
Inscribed *The Deer Slayer* (twice)/*by J.Fennimore Cooper* (twice)
1904

SD.1101.1979

309

Catalogue of garden ornaments by Liberty & Co.
17·5 × 12·5
c.1905

Includes urns and flower pots designed by Archibald Knox and Harry Silver

SE.462.1979

310

Design for a wallpaper
83·3 × 69
Watercolour and gouache on cartridge paper
c.1905

There was a renewal of interest in French eighteenth-century and Empire decorating at the turn of the century, coinciding with the popularity of Beaux-Arts architecture and the *Entente Cordiale*. In decorating, at least, it was a short-lived revival, disappearing before the First World War, but while it lasted, it provided the English middle classes with another alternative to Art Nouveau. This wallpaper scheme is based on a design of ears of wheat and trailing ribbon.

SD.1393.1979

***311**

Sketch design for a wallpaper
55·7 × 38
Pencil and watercolour on cartridge paper
c.1905

Sheet containing two differently scaled versions of the same design of stylized roses on elongated stems. Influence of C.R.Mackintosh is apparent here.

SD.1252.1979

305

311

314

316

312

Design for a cushion cover
69 × 61
Watercolour on cartridge paper
Inscribed *32387*
c.1905

Inspired by Kate Greenaway's book illustrations. Probably intended for Liberty & Co.

SD.1433.1979

313

Design for a letter heading
24 × 51·5
Pencil on detail paper
Inscribed *H.H.Lea 112 Wood Street, Cheapside, London EC*
c.1905

H.H.Lea acted as London agents for a number of French and Belgian textile manufacturers, including Leborgne, who bought more Silver Studio designs in the early 1900s than any English firm at that time.

SD.1172.1979

***314**

Design for a wallpaper
78·3 × 52·2
Watercolour on cartridge paper
Inscribed *No.32575*
c.1905

Although the style of this design is that of the late 1890s, the light colours, shaded to resemble stencilling, are typical of this date

SD.2047.1979

315

Design for a printed furnishing textile
11·5 × 9·5
Watercolour on tracing paper
Inscribed *verso 33082*
c.1905

By 1905, the taste for antiques and period textiles was becoming widespread amongst the middle classes. This design is an accurate reproduction of English seventeenth-century needlework, probably by Herbert Crofts, who specialised in period designs.

SD.2039.2979

***316**

Design for a wallpaper
46 × 34·5
Watercolour and pencil on detail paper
Inscribed *05478C*
c.1905

A very stylized version of a late eighteenth-century printed cotton. The abstraction and simplicity of these designs of the period 1900–10 had a great influence on the Continent – the baskets of leaves and fruit in this particular example anticipate French Modernist design of the 1920s.

SD.420.1978

317

Design for a wallpaper
54·5 × 43
Pencil and watercolour on detail paper
Inscribed *05307*
c.1905

Design probably for a machine-printed wallpaper and executed to resemble stencilling with gaps to reproduce the spaces left by stencil ties

SD.422.1978

318
Design for a printed furnishing textile
48·5 × 32·5
Gouache on cartridge paper
Inscribed *32951*
c.1905

An elegant, formal design of stylized thistles

SD.425.1978

***319**
Two designs for printed furnishing textiles
32·8 × 24·7 and 32·5 × 24·7
Watercolour on tracing and cartridge papers
Inscribed *05988*
1905

These designs are derived from seventeenth-century English needlework and reflect the growing taste for realistic reproductions of historic textiles at this date

SD.1481–2.1979

320
Design for a printed furnishing textile
48·7 × 46
Pastel on tracing paper
Inscribed *05437*
1905

Late English Art Nouveau design, showing the increasing stylisation which characterised avant-garde English pattern design of the period

SD.1508.1979

321
Design for a wallpaper 'crown' decoration
38 × 42
Watercolour and pencil on cartridge paper
c.1905

The 'crown' decoration was a popular but short-lived fashion of using wallpaper where filling and frieze were combined in one continuous wall length of about 4 yards. The French rose and trellis paper was typical of popular wallpaper design of this period.

SD.2029.1979

322
Woven furnishing textile
14 × 30·5
1907

Moquette manufactured in France by Fand Leborgne et Cie from Silver Studio design No.13757. The design was probably by Harry Napper, as it clearly resembles some of his work for Rottmann and Co., in the early 1900s (see 257). This is a particularly good example of formalised English Art Nouveau.

ST.15.1979

323
Block-printed linens
55·9 × 81 (mount size)
1907–8

Two colourways each of two linens produced by R.Denby & Sons of Bradford from designs by the Silver Studio. The designs show clearly the reaction away from elaborate patterns and rich colours in favour of lighter effects in the early years of the twentieth century. The two upper samples are copies of a traditional early Victorian chintz. The lower sample show the last traces of English Art Nouveau, before it became completely unfashionable, c.1910.

Ref. *Silver Studio Sales Record 1905–17*, p.79

ST.34–5.1979

324
Two designs for stencil friezes
Crayon and watercolour on cartridge paper
1907

These formalized Art Nouveau friezes were possibly intended for Rex and Harry Silver's stencilling venture and could be applied to a wide variety of materials

SD.467.1979

325
Stencil frieze
36 × 76
Distemper on paper
1908

Design of naturalistic roses and ribbons reflecting the popular taste for French Second Empire decoration

SW.1561.1979

***326**
Design for a chintz
23 × 21·5
Watercolour on detail paper
Inscribed *06766*
1907

A copy of an early Victorian chintz by Herbert Crofts

SD.1449.1979

319

326

Part Three: 1910–1939

The most remarkable feature of this period of the Studio's history is the quite astonishing variety of designs produced for textiles and wallpapers. The majority were in period styles, but when the opportunity came, the Studio was capable of supplying extremely good avant-garde work.

Until the 1930s, it was in the field of printed textiles that this versatility was best shown. After 1910, patterned wallpapers declined dramatically in popularity in upper- and middle-class houses, and until one or two firms began experimenting with new designs and materials in woven textiles in the late 1920s, most designs used by manufacturers of woven furnishing textiles were adaptations of traditional seventeeth- and eighteenth-century brocades and damasks.

The period designs produced for printed furnishing textiles fall into a number of distinct categories. Around 1910 the most popular were copies of French eighteenth- and early nineteenth-century designs, using motifs such as baskets of Sèvres roses and ribbon trellis, reflecting the renewal of interest in French decorating and architecture which occurred in the early 1900s. This phase was soon followed by copies of Early Victorian chintzes, with large brightly coloured designs of naturalistic flowers, leaves and fruit on light grounds, and by elaborate chinoiserie patterns of tropical birds, foliage and flowers. After the First World War rather more patriotic designs based on motifs from Tudor and Stuart needlework, in dark colours on a beige or cream ground, became the most popular and remained so until the 1940s. From the mid 1930s onwards the studio became famous for its productions of elegant neo-Baroque and Regency designs, in rich and subtle colour combinations. These were usually for glazed chintz and were typical of that movement which lasted until the Studio closed for a smart, whimsical eclectic style of decoration best seen in the interiors designed by Basil Ionides and Sybil Colefax, and in illustrations by Rex Whistler.

The Studio's modern designs for this period were for two totally dissimilar groups of manufacturers. On the one hand there were a small number of textile firms who carried on the traditions of the best manufacturers of the 1880s and 1890s. They used only the work of the best designers available, were prepared to be avant-garde and who took very considerable risks in the light of the serious financial crises of the 1920s and 1930s. The best known in the period 1910 to 1925 was W. Foxton. Within the Silver Studio, Harry Silver, Winifred Mold and Lewis Jones supplied designs for this firm. Because they had a Paris office, Foxton were extremely conscious of design developments in France, and the designs supplied to them by the Studio reflect this. They were characterised by the use of brilliant colour, flat stylized leaves and flowers and simple geometric patterns, such as stripes, checks, circles. The Studio sold similar designs to Morton Sundour, Franklin and Story & Co. From the late 1920s onwards, the Studio sold rather more abstract designs, inspired by Cubism and motifs from peasant art, to a few firms which were working to improve the level of woven textiles in Britain, including Donald Bros, Warner and Sons and the Edinburgh Weavers. These designs, intended for a wide variety of woven materials, were much closer to the work of the Bauhaus than to French avant-garde work, and were usually in pale colours – beige, cream, grey. These manufacturers worked closely with the Silver Studio in the production of their designs, and the Studio diaries of the 1930s record the frequent visits of their design managers.

This was in complete contrast to the other group of manufacturers for whom the Silver Studio supplied modern designs. These were the firms that manufactured cheap wallpapers and furnishing textiles. They were highly competitive and anxiously sought after the most novel effects (so long as these were not too dissimilar from last year's best-selling designs). In the early 1920s their most popular subjects were exotic Oriental or Arabian landscape scenes, in brilliant colours. After 1925, adaptations of French modern design became popular, with wallpaper and manufacturers producing at first friezes and subsequently whole lengths of wallpaper covered with soft, Fauvist flowers and leaf motifs. In the early 1930s Cubism became fashionable, in subdued colours, but with the severity of such designs modified by the addition of such disparate motifs as stylized or naturalistic flowers. By the mid 1930s, designs loosely based on the avant-garde work of France and Germany were available in a whole range of cheap printed and woven textiles and wallpapers. Almost all were in shades of brown or cream, with additions of patches of brighter colours – blue, orange, green, red. Rex Silver was reluctantly obliged to produce large quantities of these designs. The sole objective of these firms was to make as large a profit as possible; they paid their designers badly, and, because they were unsure of their exact design needs, extremely difficult to work for.

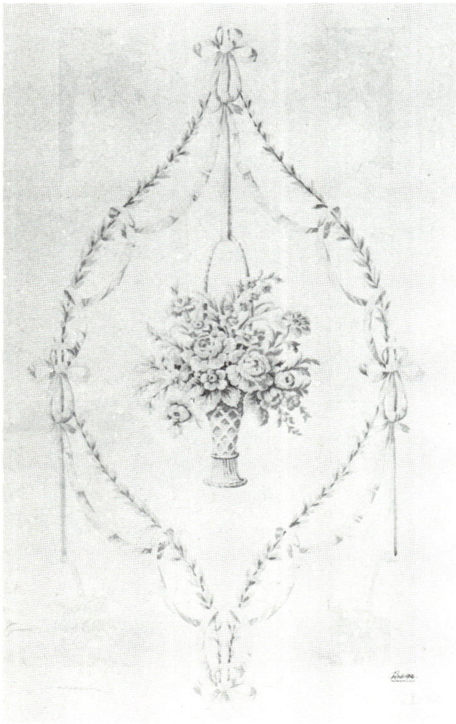

330

327

Country Life photograph of the interior of a town house
24 × 19
c.1910

Illustrations of smart interiors from journals such as *Country Life* must have had a great influence on middle-class decorating tastes in the early twentieth century, and helped encourage the use of plain walls and antique furniture

328

Pamphlet advertising the St James's Court flats, Buckingham Gate, SW1
12 × 18
c.1910

Rex Silver's first commission for a complete interior scheme came in 1913, when he designed the decorations for one of these flats for a Major McMicking

SE.505.1979

329

Printed cotton
114 × 81
c.1910

Probably designed by Herbert Crofts. This is a French Second Empire design of a type fashionable in the period 1900–15, with trailing ribbons, bunches of Sèvres roses etc., in pinks, greys, pale blue on a cream ground.

ST.56.1979

***330**

Design for a chintz
68·2 × 50·5
Watercolour and pencil on cartridge paper
Inscribed *B.363*
c.1910

This design of ribbons and baskets of Pompadour roses was typical of the French Second Empire style which formed a popular alternative to Arts and Crafts decorating in the early years of the twentieth century.

By H.C. Bareham

SD.1196.1979

331

333

***331**

Design for a chintz
34 × 24·5
Watercolour on detail paper
Inscribed on old mount *33223*
1910

This Second Empire chintz design was sold to Koechlin Baumgarten & Co., of 79 Watling Street, EC on 13 October 1910

SD.1299.1979

332

Design for a wallpaper
24·3 × 13·2
Pencil on tracing paper
Inscribed *96*
1910

Opulent design inspired by French eighteenth-century decorative art intended for an expensive wallpaper

SD.1461.1979

***333**

Design for a wallpaper
21·3 × 16·5
Pencil and watercolour on detail paper
Inscribed *148*
1910

The Silver Studio day book states that this design was based on 'Oval Chippendale Frame holding groups of flowers etc.'

SD.1462.1979

334

Design for a chintz
29·5 × 24
Watercolour on detail paper
Inscribed *32832*
1910

This design is a copy of an early Victorian chintz by Herbert Crofts. Influenced by illustrations in periodicals such as *Country Life*, old-fashioned glazed chintz, which had never gone out of fashion in large country houses, was enjoying a popular revival amongst the English middle classes.

SD.1448.1979

335

Sheet of designs from *Le Journal de la Décoration*
35 × 25
Inscribed *Le Journal de la Décoration, publication périodique/Décorations Modernes par H.Fritsch*
1911

These designs show how modern pattern design was developing on the Continent c.1910–20. These illustrations show the influence of C.R.Mackintosh, combined with brilliant colours from the Russian Ballet and Fauvism.

SE.279.1979

336

Design for a trade card
30·3 × 22·3
Pencil on detail paper
Inscribed *1911. AD/B.D.A./The Bradford Dyers Association Limited*

The Silver Studio frequently designed advertisements and trade cards for their clients. This one was executed by Harry Silver.

SD.1463.1979

***337**

Design for a chintz
30·7 × 15·3
Pencil on cartridge paper
Inscribed *275*
1912

Late eighteenth-century French designs were continuously popular over the period 1880–1910. This is a beautifully drawn example by Herbert Crofts.

SD.1465.1979

***338**

Design for a printed furnishing textile
50·2 × 48·6
Gouache on cartridge paper
Inscribed *213*
c.1912

By J.R.Doughty. This is a curious design based on Art Nouveau but with brilliant *Ballet Russe* colours.

SD.1246.1979

339

Design for a printed furnishing textile
45·5 × 45·5
Gouache on cartridge paper
c.1912

Brilliant colours showing the influence of the *Ballet Russe* productions. The C.R.Mackintosh roses, checks etc., anticipate French decorative art of the 1920s.

SD.1245.1979

337

338

***340**

Design for a chintz
24·3 × 19
Pencil, wash and coloured crayon on tracing paper
Inscribed *657*
1912

By 1912 the Silver Studio had virtually abandoned their elegant and economically late Art Nouveau designs in favour of period designs. This design was based on a section of Grinling Gibbons's carving.

SD.1445.1979

341

Design for a chintz
50 × 38
Pencil, charcoal and crayon on detail paper
Inscribed *105*
1912

This design by Herbert Crofts is based on a traditional English chintz. By 1910 English Art Nouveau was nothing more than an out-moded style. Instead of developing the abstraction of English Art Nouveau designs, as was done on the Continent, the English middle classes returned to buying textiles with designs which were reproductions of historical styles, such as this one.

SD.419.1979

***342**

Design for a printed textile
81·2 × 69·5
Watercolour on cartridge paper
Inscribed *749/21" high × 21" wide*
1913

This design by Harry Silver retains a trace of Art Nouveau, particularly in the background flowers, which are reminiscent of Harry Napper's work

SD.2000.1979

***343**

Design for a printed textile
17 × 18
Pencil and wash on tracing paper
Inscribed *No 432*
1913

Based on an Indian chintz pattern. By Harry Silver.

SD.2040.1979

There is no entry 344

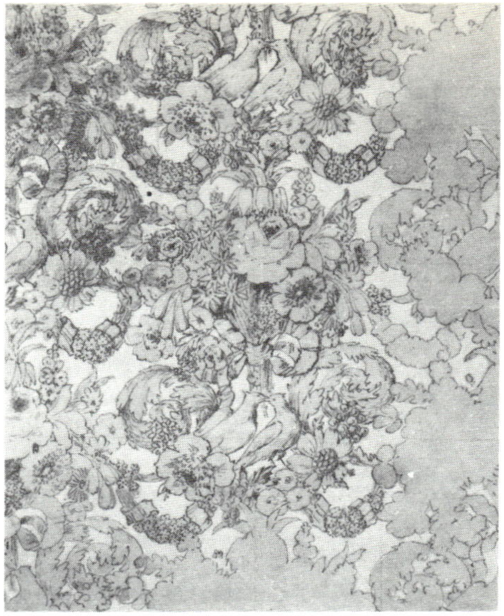
340

342

345

Design for a printed furnishing textile
23·7 × 19·2
Watercolour, gouache on cartridge paper
Inscribed *753*
1913

Harry Silver has given this design, despite its seventeenth-century needlework origins – an elegant Arts and Crafts feeling by its economical and stylized draughtsmanship

SD.1456.1979

343

347

346

Design for a cretonne
21 × 20·2
Watercolour on detail paper
Inscribed *447*
1913

An early example by Winifred Mold of an elaborate chinoiserie design of a type that was to become ubiquitous throughout the 1920s for smart furnishing textiles

SD.1452.1979

***347**

Design for a printed furnishing textile
12 × 9
Watercolour on tracing paper
Inscribed, *verso, 477*
1914

An early example of the vogue for using exotic Japanese motifs such as lanterns, pine-trees, camellias etc., for cheap textiles and wallpapers

SD.1460.1979

348

Design for an embroidered cushion cover
68 × 70
Pencil and watercolour on detail paper
Inscribed *661*
1915

By Harry Silver, who still produced some Arts and Crafts designs like this one

SD.1434.1979

349

Design for a cretonne
82·7 × 70
Watercolour and gouache on cartridge paper
Inscribed *745*
1915

By Herbert Crofts

SD.1431.1979

350

Design for a printed textile
34 × 29·5
Inscribed *1421*
1919

This design by Lewis Jones is indicative of the growing popularity of exotic Oriental subjects for textiles and wallpapers

SD.1391.1979

351

Samples of block-printed dress silks
40 × 56 (mount size)
1918–c.1925

The design of Japanese umbrellas was by Miss Winifred Mold from the Silver Studio. Silver Studio design No.1530, executed in 1918 and printed for Liberty.

ST.8.1979

362

352

Glazed chintz
184 × 65
c.1850

Early Victorian block-printed chintz with a design of large, full-blown peonies and trailing leaves, in strong reds and greens on a cream ground. Acquired by Rex Silver probably to use as a source of inspiration for printed textile designs in the 1920s, when there was a vogue for early Victorian chintz designs.

ST.57.1979

353

Design for a printed textile
20 × 17
Watercolour on tracing paper
Inscribed *1987/24" × 28" W/8 cols*
1920

An elegant period design by Herbert Crofts, with late eighteenth-century birds. Typical of the period designs that the Silver Studio were producing from 1910 to 1930.

SD.2035.1979

354

Block-printed linen
38 × 46
c.1920

Although this is an English textile (probably printed by Foxton) it reflects fashionable European taste, with its overtones of Cubism, and check background. The fabric was labelled *Futurist* – a term which was used in England from c.1915 onwards to describe all abstract pattern designs, regardless of their relationship to the art movement which inspired the name. Minnie McLeish wrote in the *Journal of the DIA* in 1919: '... these modest little patterns, as old as the hills, have been called *Futurist* and *Dazzle* to distinguish their modern wildness from old time staidness!' From c.1925 until the Second World War avant-garde pattern designs were called in trade journals *Modernist* just as in the 1950s they were called *Contemporary*.

ST.33.1979

355

Block-printed cotton
46 × 35·5
c.1920

The drawing and brilliant colours would indicate that this textile is French. Its presence in the Silver Studio Collection was probably as source material for a range of similar designs for printed cottons designed by Winifred Mold. An almost identical textile to this one was produced by Foxton's from Silver Studio design No.988 in 1921 (illustrated in W.G.Paulson Townsend: *Modern Decorative Art in England*, London, 1922, p.87, fig.81).

ST.31.1979

356

Two advertisements for *Devon* fires
20 × 30
c.1920

These were produced by Candy & Co. Ltd. The left-hand fireplace was designed by Sir Edwin Lutyens. Both illustrations are excellent examples of the ideal middle-class sitting room of the 1920s. One is rather Georgian, the other blatantly neo-Tudor, both place emphasis on the use of period furniture and plain walls.

SE.474.1979

357

Printed cotton
64·5 × 76
c.1920

Opulent neo-late eighteenth-century design, probably by Miss Winifred Mold, with exotic birds, baskets of fruit, strawberries, vines and passion flowers, in shades of plum red, pale grey and beige on grey ground

ST.54.1979

358

Printed linen
57 × 132
Illustrated in *Modern Decorative Art in England* by W.G.Paulson Townsend, p.93, 1922
c.1920

Design of dense foliage framing landscape panels, entitled *Sunshine and Shadow*. Manufactured by the Ramsden Wood Print Works Ltd.

ST.61.1979

359

Cotton furnishing textile
48 × 77·5
Block-printed cotton
c.1920

Probably produced by W.Foxton Ltd, and inspired by contemporary French decorative art, with a design of vertical panels, some containing stylized flowers. In shades of blue, yellow, red, orange and black.

ST.63.1979

360

Two plates (Nos.6 and 20) from E.A.Seguy's *Suggestions*
44·5 × 32
Inscribed *Suggestions/for/Stuffs and Carpets*
c.1920

The Silver Studio made frequent use of these pochoir-printed plates for their avant-garde designs in the 1930s. John Churton's rug designs in particular were based on motifs from these plates, but with drastically altered colours.

SE.481.1979

***361**

Design for a printed furnishing textile
84 × 83·5
Inscribed *868*
1922

This design by Herbert Crofts was sold to Liberty in 1922

SD.448.1978

***362**

Design for a printed furnishing textile
73 × 60
Gouache, watercolour and pencil on detail paper
Inscribed *2424*
1922

Designed by J.R.Houghton, who presumably sold this design via the Silver Studio as he had left in 1902 to start his own studio in Essex. Note the black ground which was a popular feature of printed textiles in the 1920s and 1930s. Based on eighteenth-century chinoiserie, which was a major source of period design for textiles from 1910 onwards.

SD.1193.1979

363

Four plates from Benedictus's *Variations*
each 47·5 × 37
1924

Like the work of Seguy, these plates were used as source material by the Silver Studio in the late 1920s and 1930s

SE.482.1979

***364**

Design for a printed furnishing textile, *The Garden of Allah*
30·5 × 23·7
Gouache on cartridge paper
Inscribed *2724*
1924

Designed by Winifred Mold. This design reflects the popular taste for a romanticised view of the Near-East, encouraged by plays such as *Kismet*, *Hassan*, the discovery of the tomb of Tutankhamen, in 1922, and above all the cinema and E. M. Hull's novel *The Sheik*.

SD.1302.1979

***365**

Design for a printed furnishing textile
81 × 68
Watercolour on tracing paper
Inscribed with colour code *2629*
1923

This design by Lewis Jones was doubtless inspired by the discovery by Lord Carnarvon of the tomb of Tutankhamen. Note the contemporary French influence visible in the use of broad stripes and decorative panels.

SD.453.1979

***366**

Design for a printed furnishing textile
83·5 × 72·5
Gouache on tracing paper
Inscribed *2988*
1924

This design by Madeleine Lawrence is typical of the vogue for exotic Oriental landscape patterns in the early 1920s

SD.450.1978

367

Printed cotton
13 × 22
c.1925

A copy of an early nineteenth-century design of large flowers and acanthus scrolls in rich colours

ST.44.1979

364

365

366

368

370

***368**

Design for a bedspread
70 × 63·8
Watercolour and pencil on cartridge paper
Inscribed *3747*
1925

A simple Arts and Crafts style continued to be popular in the 1920s for nursery textiles and wallpaper and for children's book illustrations. This example is by Herbert Crofts.

SD.1191.1979

369

Wallpaper pattern book
30·5 × 23·5
Inscribed on cover *Kleurverzameling*
c.1925

Although this pattern book was produced in Holland, most of the wallpapers included are French – a number are designed by Paul Poiret's 'Atelier Martine'. Rex Silver probably acquired this book to use as source material for Silver Studio textile designs.

SW.158.1977

***370**

Design for a printed furnishing textile
67 × 61·2
Gouache on cartridge paper
Inscribed *16052* in pencil *154*
1925

This design was executed after Rex Silver's visit to the Paris Exhibition of 1925 and shows the influence of contemporary French textile design

SD.1334.1979

371
Cut-out wallpaper frieze
26 × 42
Inscribed, *verso, A.55989*
c.1925

SW.938.1977

372
Sheet of designs for screens and panels
35 × 24·5
c.1925

Continental designs such as these by the German designer Erich Lindenan were used in England as the source for many designs for Modernist textiles and wallpapers in the 1930s

SE.475.1979

***373**
Cut-out wallpaper border
13·5 × 42
Inscribed, *verso, A.55461*
c.1925

Design of romantic chinoiserie with paper lanterns, birds and leaves, in six colours

SW.940.1977

374
Wallpaper pattern book produced by W. Froy
37 × 53·2
Inscribed, on cover, *Artistic Wallpapers/Season 1925*
1925

SW.30.1976

375
Design for a wallpaper
55 × 37·5
Gouache, gold paint and pencil on cartridge paper
Inscribed in pencil *F/Drawn for Wallpaper 10½ × 15″*
c.1925

Trailing, all-over chintz designs were popular for cheap wallpapers during the late 1920s and 1930s

SD.1559.1979

376
Sketch for a printed textile design
106 × 55
Oil paint on brown sugar paper
Signed *L. Silas*
c.1925

Louis Silas designed for both Arthur and Rex Silver. This romantic, theatrical sketch was probably intended as source material for a chintz.

SD.2057.1979

373

378

377
Design for a chintz
100·5 × 84
Gouache, watercolour on cartridge paper
Inscribed *3778*
1925

An early design by Frank Price showing his ability to make designs based on late eighteenth-century ornament – a talent he was to develop during the 1930s and 1940s

SD.2001.1979

***378**
Design for a printed furnishing textile
35·5 × 25·5
Watercolour, gouache on detail paper
Inscribed *3266*
1925

A typical example of a Silver Studio design (by Lewis Jones) showing the influence of contemporary French decorative art, which can be seen in the check stripe and stylized roses

SD.1459.1979

379

***379**
Design for a wallpaper
24·9 × 21·5
Watercolour and pencil on grey cartridge paper
Inscribed *3785*
1925

Executed by R.J. Doughty, and shows the English middle-class taste in the 1920s for period decoration – the motifs in this example derive from Stuart needlework

SD.403.1978

380
Samples of block-printed dress silks
40 × 56 cms (mount size)
c.1925

Examples of the brilliant colours and Oriental-inspired designs used for smart dress silks in the early 1920s

ST.9.1979

***381**
Design for a wallpaper
65·5 × 52
Gouache on cartridge paper
Inscribed *4435*
1926

By R.J. Doughty

SD.2010.1979

382
Wallpaper pattern book
25·5 × 40·7
Inscribed, on cover, *New Wall-Papers/1926–7*
1926

Most of the samples seem to be by Lightbown & Aspinall and Potters of Darwen, and certainly represent the cheaper end of the wallpaper market

SW.35.1976

***383**
Design for a cut-out wallpaper frieze
Gouache, watercolour and pencil on cartridge paper
Inscribed *3900*
1926

Cut-out wallpaper friezes became more elaborate as the 1920s progressed (see 395). This design features the brilliant colours popular in the early 1920s and the equally fashionable Chinese lantern.

SD.478.1979

***384**
Design for a wallpaper
58·2 × 46
Gouache on cartridge paper
Inscribed *4377*
1926

This type of dense all-over wallpaper design, known in the trade as 'verdure' was extremely popular in the 1920s and 1930s

SD.1515(a).1979

381

383

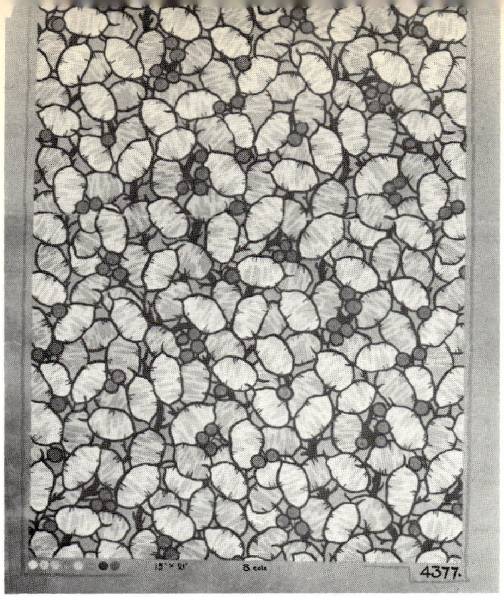

384

385

***385**

Design for a wallpaper
23·3 × 21·5
Watercolour on detail paper
Inscribed *4935B*
1926

SD.1446.1979

***386**

Design for a wallpaper or printed textile
81·2 × 60·5
Gouache on cartridge paper
Inscribed *4891*
1927

Note the use of rich, French colours – red, green, violet, black and so on

SD.1251.1979

386

4615
SILVER STUDIO COLL.

***387**
Design for a chintz
82 × 63·2
Gouache on cartridge paper
Inscribed *4618* with colour code
1927

By Madeleine Lawrence. Note the fashionable black ground.

SD.1250.1979

388
Design for a wallpaper
60 × 83
Gouache on cartridge paper
Inscribed *4809*
1927

By Edwin Parker

SD.1548.1979

389
Printed dress silk *Miniature Peacock*
20 × 53
Block-printed silk
1927

Designed by Edwin Parker for Simons: The block was subsequently bought by Warner and printed at Dartford in 1930.

Lent by Warner Sons Ltd (No.WS369)

390
Dress silk *Small Tulips*
24 × 82
Block-printed silk
1927

From Silver Studio design No.5000 by Edwin Parker. The design was bought by Simons in 1927 and the block subsequently purchased by Warner in 1930 and printed at Dartford.

Lent by Warner and Sons Ltd (No.WS279)

391
Design for a chintz
50 × 40
Watercolour on cartridge paper
Inscribed *4657*
1927

Chinoiserie designs were enormously popular in the 1920s for all classes of decorating. This one, by Madeleine Lawrence, appears to be copied from an early nineteenth-century chintz.

SD.434.1978

392
Design for a furnishing textile
45·5 × 45·5
Gouache and gold paint on cartridge paper
Inscribed in pencil *141P/4643*
1927

This design closely relates to the most fashionable French pattern designs of this date. The opulent use of gold and sophisticated draughtsmanship were probably too extreme for English manufacturers. Madeleine Lawrence (who produced this design) later made a speciality of producing designs for Liberty dress fabrics.

SD.1489.1979

***393**
Block-printed wallpaper corner
23·5 × 25·5
c.1928

Rex Silver had this design adapted for use as a dress silk

SW.953.1977

394
Wallpaper border
12 × 53·5
Inscribed, *verso*, in Rex Silver's hand, *We re-arranged/this entirely and introduced squares*
c.1928

Block-printed wallpaper border with design of squares, leaves and fruit, re-designed by the Silver Studio

SW.947.1977

***395**
Block-printed wallpaper corner
40 × 33
Inscribed, *verso*, with the trade mark for Hayward & Sons and *Butterfly Corner F.8*
c.1928

Hayward & Sons had an excellent reputation for the quality of their wallpaper printing and this frieze would have been expensive to buy. However, these cut-out wallpaper decorations were very much confined to lower-middle- and working-class home decoration.

SW.958.1977

396
Design for a printed furnishing textile
19·5 × 18
Gouache and pencil on tracing paper
Inscribed *6092*
1928

Design by Herbert Crofts based on seventeenth-century English needlework

SD.2038.1979

393

395

397

SILVER STUDIO COLL.
5923.

***397**

Design for a dress silk
21 × 16·2
Watercolour, gouache on cartridge paper
Inscribed *5580*
1928

A design for a dress silk inspired by contemporary French pattern design

SD.1454.1979

***398**

Design for a printed furnishing textile
21·5 × 20·5
Watercolour on detail paper
Inscribed *5923*
1928

Given a sympathetic and enlightened manufacturer, the Silver Studio could turn out work as good as any of their French contemporaries. This charming design of a stylized basket of flowers in fresh blues and pinks on a white ground was executed by Miss Winifred Mold.

SD.1447.1979

The following designs (399–400) are by a Monsieur Dupont who was apprenticed to the Silver Studio for a year in 1929. He sent some of his work to Rex for inspection before his arrival in England (see the Silver Studio Diary for 1929, 15th March).

***399**

Design for a wallpaper
61·2 × 49·3
Gouache and watercolour on cartridge paper
1929

The colours – reds, browns, etc. – used in this design were to become fashionable in England in the early 1930s

SD.1244.1979

400

Design for a printed cotton
71·5 × 60
Gouache on cartridge paper
Inscribed *10 × 16/11 couleurs*
1929

SD.1267.1979

401

Design for a printed cotton
46 × 38
Gouache, watercolour on detail paper
Inscribed *194L*
1924

Traditional chintz design by Madeleine Lawrence

SD.1253.1979

402

Design for a wallpaper
50·5 × 40
Gouache on cartridge paper
Inscribed *53401/29625*
1929

SD.1488.1979

403

Design for a printed textile
23 × 18·5
Pencil and wash on tracing paper
Inscribed *English Needlework/6369*
1929

This type of imitation-Jacobean needlework design was the main support of the Silver Studio during the 1920s and 1930s. It was produced in endless variations for a wide range of textiles and sometimes for wallpaper.

SD.2036.1979

404

Design for a printed furnishing textile
20 × 16
Pencil and wash on tracing paper
Inscribed *Portuguese/17th Century/6360A*
1929

Although this design is based on seventeenth-century Portuguese embroidery, it manages to convey a 'Tudorbethan' effect in keeping with contemporary middle-class taste

SD.2037.1979

***405**

Design for a printed furnishing textile
43·5 × 40
Watercolour on cartridge paper
Inscribed *6480A*
1929

Design shows a strong French influence in the use of stylized flowers and fruit

SD.449.1978

***406**

Design for a printed furnishing linen
43·3 × 30·6
Watercolour on cartridge paper
1929

This design by Lewis Jones was based on a piece of antique Spanish leather from the Victoria and Albert Museum and painted in faded colours in order to render the finished textile suitable for use in conjunction with antique or reproduction furniture

SD.1492.1979

399

405

406

407

Design for a trade card/map showing the situation of the Silver Studio
14 × 20
Pencil and pen and ink on card
Annotated in Rex Silver's hand
c.1930

This was probably designed and executed by Rex Silver

SE.515.1979

408

Printed cotton
94 × 77
c.1930

Roller-printed cotton with design of stylized poppies in a vase. Printed in strong colours – reds, yellows, green and blue, on a coffee ground.

ST.55.1979

409

Dress silk
24 × 86
c.1930

Block-printed dress silk produced by Liberty & Co, from a design by Madeleine Lawrence. This type of design was originally executed by the Silver Studio for wallpapers, but discovered by Liberty and used for an extremely popular series of dress fabrics.

ST.45.1979

410

Printed linen
43 × 79
c.1930

Roller-printed linen with design of geometric shapes and stylized flowers

ST.60.1979

411

Cut-out wallpaper border
12·2 × 32·5
Inscribed, *verso*, *Cut Out 90818 = 4 over*
c.1930

An excellent example of a 'Jazz' Modernist design of the early 1930s, derived from Cubist and Egyptian motifs and usually associated with the decoration of Odeon cinemas

SW.949.1977

412

Block-printed linen, *The Argosy*
70 × 56
1930

Designed by Herbert Crofts in 1929 and printed by Warner at Dartford in 1930

Lent by Warner and Sons Ltd (No.WS388)

413

Glazed chintz, *Zanzibar*
58 × 78·5
Roller-printed cotton
1930

Designed by Lewis Jones in 1929 and printed for Warner by Stead McAlpin. Based on a French *Toile de Jouy*.

Lent by Warner and Sons Ltd (No.CC1895)

414

Printed dress silk, *Bubbles*
14 × 13
Block-printed silk
1930

This was designed by the Silver Studio in 1919 and sold to Simons, who, in turn, sold the block to Warner in 1930

Lent by Warner and Sons Ltd (No.WS284)

415

Dress silk, *Floral Medley*
44 × 65
Block-printed dress silk
1930

The design was bought by Simons from the Silver Studio in 1928 and the block subsequently bought by Warner in 1930

Lent by Warner and Sons Ltd (No.WS282)

416

Dress cotton, *Indian Pink*
34 × 65·5
Block-printed cotton
1930

Designed by Arthur Freeman of the Silver Studio in 1927 and subsequently bought by Warner from Simons in 1930. Another version of this design was sold for wallpaper.

Lent by Warner & Sons Ltd (No.WS368)

417

Block-printed cotton, *Interlace*
53·5 × 83
1930

Designed by Harry Napper in 1919, sold to Simons and subsequently printed by Warner

Lent by Warner & Sons Ltd (No.000000)

418

Block-printed linen, *Zebra Stripes*
20 × 73
1930

Designed by Lewis Jones of the Silver Studio in 1919

Lent by Warner & Sons Ltd

419

Printed cotton furnishing textile, *Check Border*
12 × 34
Block-printed cotton
1930

Designed in 1919 by Lewis Jones and produced by Warner in 1930

Lent by Warner & Sons Ltd (No.WS333)

420

Block-printed linen, *Lily Auratum*
147 × 45
1930

Designed by Miss Winifred Mold of the Silver Studio in 1925 and produced by Warner in 1930

Lent by Warner & Sons Ltd

421

Still-life sketch of cottage flowers before an antique looking-glass
75 × 62
Watercolour on cartridge paper
c.1930

By H.C.Bareham. Bareham had occasionally produced designs for the Silver Studio from 1903 onwards, and from 1942 worked regularly for Rex Silver (but as an outside designer) until the Studio closed. This watercolour can be seen almost as a homage to middle-class furnishing taste in the 1920s – Bristol glass vase, antique looking-glass – even the colours, with tertiary shades predominating.

SD.2020.1979

422

Block-printed cotton
48 × 44·5
c.1930

This textile shows an attempt to produce a modern version of a traditional eighteenth-century chintz design. If the manufacturers had risked using brilliant French colours, it might have been successful. Instead they have used subdued colours with not very satisfactory results.

ST.28.1979

423

Block-printed cotton voile
20 × 28·5
c.1930

When not restricted by manufacturers' demands, the Silver Studio was capable of producing original and sensitively coloured designs

ST.29.1979

424

Machine-printed cotton
45 × 45
c.1930

Designed by George Willis of the Silver Studio. This type of lush, naturalistic floral design was particularly fashionable in the United States in the 1920s and derives from mid nineteenth-century English chintzes.

ST.20.1979

425

Machine-printed cotton
44·5 × 46·5
1931

Cotton furnishing textile designed by George Willis of the Silver Studio, and derived from a late eighteenth-century French chintz. Manufactured in the United States by Barmac Prints.

ST.19.1979

426

Crepe dress fabric
23 × 48
c.1930

An example of a 1920s French Modernist design used for a Liberty dress fabric

ST.10.1979

***427**

Design for a wallpaper corner
59 × 82
Gouache on tracing paper
Inscribed *7707A*
1932

This design by G.H.Willis is an excellent example of French Modernist design adapted to cheap English wallpaper

SD.446.1978

427

428

429

***428**

Design for a furnishing textile
60·6 × 52
Watercolour on detail paper
Inscribed *8003A*
1932

Designed by Lewis Jones of the Silver Studio. Note the fashionable colours – orange, brown on beige ground.

SD.23.1978

***429**

Design for a printed furnishing textile
58 × 50·5
Gouache on cartridge paper
Inscribed *8003*
1932

Design adapted from a plate by Seguy of the early 1920s, and it serves to indicate the continuing popularity in England of French decorative art of the 1920s, especially for cheaper textiles and wallpaper

SD.447.1978

432

430

John Hawkins Catalogue p.15
21 × 13·5
1933

The three right-hand illustrations on p.15 were all designed by various members of the Silver Studio staff

SE.471.1979

431

Hampton's Catalogue, *Decoration of the House Beautiful*, pp.82–3
1933

Examples of Modernist wallpaper corners and friezes of a type produced by the Silver Studio in the early 1930s

SE.470.1979

***432**

Design for a woven textile
37 × 33·5
Pencil and watercolour on detail paper
Inscribed *8508B*
1933

This Cubist design by Arthur Hogg is unusual for the date in its use of strong, clear colours at a time when rather subdued tones were fashionable

SD.424.1978

433

Design for a woven textile
42 × 32
Watercolour and pencil on detail paper
Inscribed *8508*
1933

Whilst the influence of French designers such as Sonia Delaunay is very apparent in this design, the subdued colours used here are typically English

SD.423.1978

434

Woven wool moquette
26 × 19
1933

An English interpretation of French Modernist design

ST.23(a).1979

435

Woven wool moquette
24·5 × 20·5
1933

Avant-garde designs were frequently used for woven textiles in the 1930s. Whilst firms like Donald Bros and Morton Sundour produced excellent work, the cheaper manufacturers produced less satisfactory results, partly through unimaginative colouring.

ST.23(b).1979

437

The *Coverdale* chintz
83 × 74·5
Roller-printed glazed cotton
1934

Designed by Geoffrey Willis of the Silver Studio for Warner and printed by Stead McAlpin

Lent by Warner & Sons Ltd (No.S/4056)

438

John Hawkins Catalogue, p.25
21 × 13·5
1934

The dress fabrics on p.25 were all by the Silver Studio. John Hawkins Ltd, bought many designs from the Silver Studio in the 1930s. They supplied good-quality textiles by mail order and successfully produced well-designed dress fabrics much influenced by Liberty prints.

SE.470.1979

439

Printed linen
47 × 74
1934

Block-printed linen furnishing textile from Silver Studio design No.9228. The fact that a manufacturer was prepared to produce an expensive textile like this one with a Cubist design is indicative of the growing middle-class interest in modern design durng the 1930s.

ST.14.1979

The following textile designs (440–51) are by John Churton, who had come to work for the Silver Studio as a salesman, but whose talent for avant-garde pattern design was such that Rex Silver quickly employed him as a full-time designer. His work was much influenced by French pattern design of the 1920s, but at his best he showed highly original draughtsmanship and a sensitive use of colour. Unfortunately he contracted tuberculosis and was obliged to leave the Studio in November 1934.

***440**

Design for a woven textile
48·5 × 42·6
Watercolour on detail paper
Inscribed *12½w × 13h/9544*
1934

In subtle shades of browns, yellows with grey and black

SD.2022.1979

***441**

Design for a woven textile
67·2 × 50
Gouache on sugar paper
Inscribed *12½″w × 8″H/9546*
1934

In shades of brown, white on blue/grey sugar paper

SD.2019.1979

***442**

Design for a printed furnishing textile
48 × 44·2
Gouache on detail paper
Inscribed *9316/H*
1934

In shades of brown, orange, cream, green

SD.2021.1979

***443**

Design for a printed furnishing textile
57·4 × 42
Gouache on detail paper
Inscribed *9301*
1934

Pinks and browns with green and orange

SD.2026.1979

***444**

Design for a woven textile
58·5 × 47·5
Gouache on sugar paper
Inscribed *9239*
1934

SD.435.1978

***445** + colour plate III,a,b,d

Nine designs for rugs
Various sizes
Gouache and pencil on cartridge paper
1934

These rug designs by John Churton were all inspired by the work of Modernist French designers such as Benedictus, but unlike the brilliantly coloured works of French designers, these carpets are in rather sombre shades

SD.454–SD.455.1978
SD.468–SD.474.1979

***446**

Design for a rug
35·9 × 26·8
Watercolour on cartridge paper
Inscribed *9470A*
1934

SD.400.1978

447

Design for a rug
32·5 × 26
Watercolour and gouache on cartridge paper
Inscribed *9440*
1934

SD.404.1970

448

Design for a rug
33·3 × 25·5
Watercolour on cartridge paper
Inscribed *9400*
1934

SD.401.1978

440

441

442

443

444

445

445

445

446

449

***449**

Design for a printed furnishing textile
36·6 × 40
Gouache on cartridge paper
Inscribed *9473*
1934

Design based on abstract treatment of tree forms

SD.1466.1979

450

Design for a rug
33 × 27·5
Gouache on cartridge paper
Inscribed *9382*
1934

By John Churton

SD.2105.1979

451

Three trial rug designs
41 × 56 (mount size)
Gouache on cartridge paper
Inscribed: on centre design *9398*, on right-hand design *9521*
1934

By John Churton

SD.2104.1979

***452**

Design for a tie silk
44·5 × 31
Gouache on cartridge paper
Inscribed *T221*
c.1935

Note the sensitive juxtaposition of colours in this design, which was characteristic of the Silver Studio's designs for dress silks in the 1930s

SD.433.1978

453

Glazed chintz
126 × 79·5
1934

Manufactured by Story & Co, from a design by Lewis Jones. Illustrated in *British Textile Designers of Today* by H.G. Hayes Marshall, 1939, p.247.

ST.49.1979

454

Design for a dress silk
19·5 × 17·2
Watercolour on cartridge paper
Inscribed *9510A*
1934

Although the Scandinavian influence in design did not become totally widespread until after the Second World War, this is an early example of a dress silk by Edwin Jeffrey which shows this important influence

SD.1453.1979

455

Design for a printed furnishing textile
66·8 × 56·5
Watercolour on cartridge paper
Inscribed *16" high × 14½" wide/8922*
1934

An ususual example for the date of a Cubist design by Arthur Freeman which incorporates bright colours – this at a time when subdued colours were still the height of fashion

SD.2011.1979

456

Design for a carpet
34·4 × 26·2
Watercolour on cartridge paper
Inscribed *9441*
1934

Executed by Edwin Parker

SD.402.1978

457

Warp-printed furnishing textile
31 × 37
1934

Cubist-designed warp-printed furnishing textile from Silver Studio design No.8938 by Herbert Crofts

ST.18.1979

458

Printed cotton
37 × 72
c.1935

Roller-printed cotton with a design of geometrical shapes and stylized flowers, in red, blue, orange and dark brown on mid-brown ground. This is typical of the cheap 'Jazz' style furnishing textiles of the 1930s.

ST.62.1979

452

459

Glazed chintz
98 × 133
c.1935

By Lewis Jones of the Silver Studio. Tudor and Regency revival motifs are combined in this design made up of a rope trellis framing oval panels depicting Tudor galleons. In light colours on a chocolate-brown ground.

ST.59.1979

460

Printed linen
102 × 79
c.1935

Tudor revival design of galleons, Francis Drake(?) playing bowls and large stylized flowers, all on natural linen ground

ST.53.1979

461

Printed linen
46·5 × 78
c.1935

The motifs for this design are taken from Near-Eastern tribal carpets. This is a good example of the Silver Studio's work for avant-garde manufacturers in the 1930s.

ST.47.1979

466

471

462

Five colourways of a glazed chintz
56 × 81 (mount size)
c.1935

Delicate design of flowers in fresh colours on white ground, by Madeleine Lawrence, and possibly for Liberty & Co.

ST.46.1979

463

Catalogue of Catesby Carpets and Linoleums
22 × 17
Inscribed, on cover, *For Cottage or Mansion*
c.1935

Note how in Britain dull browns, oranges, terracotta etc., were used for Modernist patterns

SE.465.1979

464

Paton and Baldwin Catalogue of patterns for home-made rugs, pp.4–5
24·5 × 18
Inscribed, on cover, *Rugcraft/6^d/Fifth edition*
c.1935

Rug-making was a popular domestic pastime in the 1930s. It is probable that some of the Silver Studio's Modernist rug designs were intended for this firm.

SE.464.1979

465

Three sheets of Modernist designs used for Axminster rugs
each 15 × 25
c.1935

Produced by Catesby Ltd. Note the subdued use of tertiary colours.

SE.467.1979

***466**

Design for a printed furnishing textile
41·5 × 46·6
Gouache on detail paper
Inscribed *9785*
1935

SD.1220(b).1979

467

Design for a woven textile
58·5 × 46·7
Charcoal on tracing paper
1935

SD.1514.1979

468

An illustration of a cut-out wallpaper decoration
29·5 × 18·8
Inscribed *The Savoy*
c.1935

This illustration of a wallpaper decoration by Sanderson is an excellent example of popularised Cubism. Note the confused interior where a number of different styles have been somewhat unhappily juxtaposed – a Spanish Baroque bed, neo-Tudor bedside table, Persian rug and a Chinese vase table lamp.

SE.525.1979

469

An illustration of a cut-out wallpaper decoration
Inscribed *The Midhurst/Sanderson*
c.1935

A good example of the colours fashionable in working-class and lower middle-class houses in the 1930s. Often known as 'Autumn Tints' they covered an enormous range of browns, reds and orange sometimes juxtaposed with green. (See 470, 474.)

SE.526.1979

470

An illustration of a cut-out wallpaper decoration
20·3 × 13·3
Inscribed *The Tintern Decoration*
c.1935

This was manufactured by Sanderson Wallpapers

SE.524.1979

***471**

Design for a wallpaper
68 × 66
Gouache on cartridge paper
Inscribed *9856*
1935

Although Nikolaus Pevsner was highly critical of English designers in the 1930s who used Cubism for pattern design without understanding the underlying principles, this example shows both good draughtsmanship and a sensitive use of colour. Greens, oranges and gold were particularly fashionable colours for furnishing textiles and wallpapers in the late 1930s. (This was true also in France, as well as in England.)

SD.437.1978

472

Three designs for wallpaper borders
82 × 63
Each inscribed with a design number
1935

These three Modernist wallpaper border designs were executed by Edwin Parker

SD.438.1978

***473**

Design for a wallpaper border
23·5 × 45
Watercolour on cartridge paper
Inscribed *9950*
1935

By Edwin Parker, in shades of brown, rust, dull green and gold

SD.2034.1979

474
Five illustrations of interiors using Sanderson wallpapers
each 20·3 × 13·3
c.1935

Illustrated examples of Sanderson cut-out wallpaper borders and corners, showing the limited range of browns – often referred to as 'Autumn Tints' fashionable for English suburban decoration at this time

SD.1475(a) to SD.1480.1979

***475**
Design for a damask border
20·5 × 61·5
Watercolour and gouache on cartridge paper
Inscribed *9766*
1935

Design derives from French decorative art of the 1920s. Note the use of brilliant *Ballet Russe* colours.

SD.436.1978

476
Roller-printed cotton
19 × 29
c.1935

Black grounds for both dress and furnishing textiles were extremely popular in the late 1920s and 1930s. This richly coloured dress fabric was probably produced by Liberty & Co.

ST.22.1979

473

477
Warp-printed furnishing textile
38 × 33·5
c.1935

The Prince of Wales' Feathers was a popular motif in the 1930s, indicative of the growing interest in the Regency period

ST.13.1979

478
Woven furnishing textile
31 × 33·5
c.1935

An early example of a simple, Scandinavian-influenced design by Lewis Jones of the Silver Studio

ST.11.1979

479
Woven wool moquette
30·5 × 28
1935

Upholstery moquette from a design by Lewis Jones of the Silver Studio (design No.9859, executed in 1935). Although the design is similar to avant-garde work being produced in France and Germany at this time, the sombre colour scheme is typical of cheap English furnishing textiles and wallpapers of the mid-1930s.

ST.32.1979

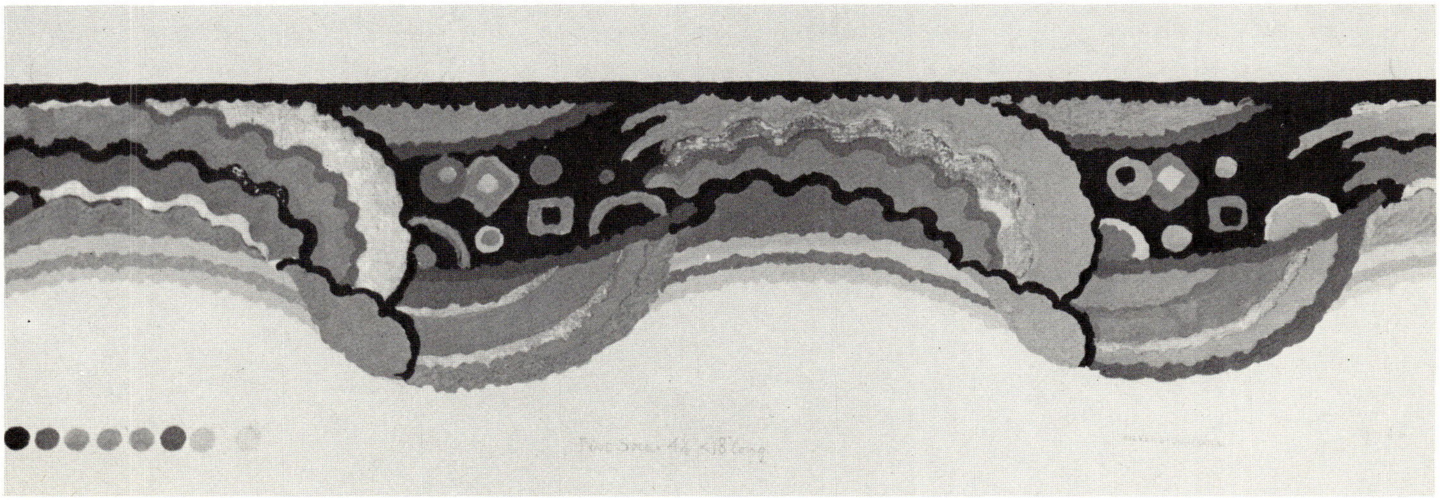

475

480

Glazed chintz
91 × 125
1937

Designed by Lewis Jones (Silver Studio design No.112112). This is a good example of the smart 1930s taste for Regency decorating. Note the colours – beige on deep salmon.

ST.48.1979

481

Rosebank Fabrics Catalogue
21·5 × 14
1937

No.6153 is from a design by Lewis Jones of the Silver Studio for Rosebank Fabrics (produced by Turnbull and Stockdale)

SE.469.1979

***482**

Design for a Liberty dress fabric
Pen and wash on detail paper
Inscribed *11264*
1937

This design was by Madeleine Lawrence, who frequently executed Silver Studio designs for Liberty's. This is typical of Silver Studio dress fabric designs of the 1930s – small naturalistic flowers in subtle colours on a light ground.

SD.481.1979

483

Catalogue of Catesby's Linoleum Patterns
22 × 18
Inscribed, on cover, *Catesby's Colourful Cork Lino*
1938

An interesting range of Modernist designs used here for cheap linoleum

SE.466.1979

484

Exhibition card showing examples of Edinburgh Weavers' Textiles produced for Gordon Russell
14·5 × 36
1938

The Silver Studio supplied several designs to the Edinburgh Weavers in the 1930s. These simple, elegant designs form an interesting contrast with the Hollywood modern designs used for cheap textiles and wallpapers.

SE.468.1979

***485**

Five designs for carpets
each approximately 70 × 45
1938

By Lewis Jones. These are typical of the rather weak Cubist designs that characterised much cheap, fashionable pattern designs in England in the 1930s. The use of pale colours was probably the influence of contemporary German textiles, which were always in a more subdued palette than those of the French.

SD.1505–15(b).1979

The following designs (486–8) were purchased by Rex Silver from Franklin and Franklin (formerly Auerbach, Franklin) in 1938, as the firm was closing down. They would appear to date from the period 1930–5, and presumably Rex Silver intended to adapt them for re-sale. Although avant-garde, they lacked the subtlety of the best Silver Studio work of the period.

***486**

Design for a printed cotton
75 × 56
Watercolour and gouaches on detail paper
Inscribed *(6¼" × 10" repeat)/A44/K2429*
1934

SD.2024.1979

***487**

Design for a printed dress fabric
73·5 × 47
Gouache on cartridge paper
Inscribed with colour notes and *K2376*
c.1935

SD.1242.1979

488

Design for a woven textile
73·8 × 53·2
Gouache and pencil on cartridge paper
Inscribed *2641/3wps 2wfts/12½" wide/K2364*
c.1935

SD.1269.1979

482

485

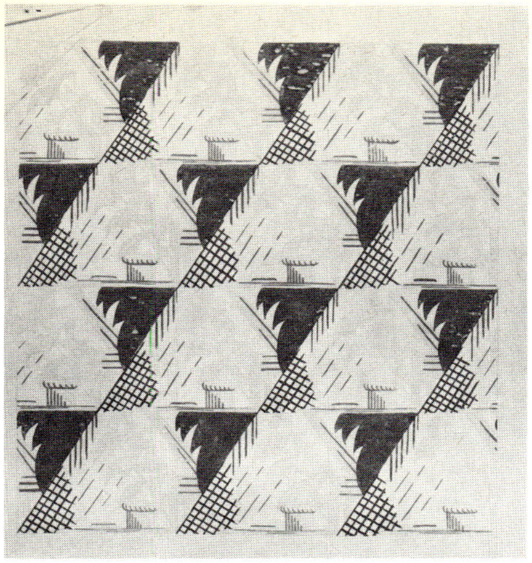

486

487

489

Six cut-out wallpaper borders
Block-printed in distemper on paper
c.1930–5

Although these cut-out borders were expensive, they were fashionable only in working- and lower-middle-class houses, where they were used in conjunction with a plain, often textured wallpaper (see 474 for illustrations of these borders in situ)

SW.1002.1977
SW.1011.1077
SW.1007.1977
SW.1010.1977
SW.1008.1977
SW.1004.1077

490

Four wallpapers
c.1930–5

Machine-printed and manufactured by Crown Wallpapers. These are good examples of Cubist patterns used for very cheap wallpapers. Note the emphasis on tertiary colours.

SW.722–SW.725.1977

491

Design for a printed textile
55·4 × 46·2
Gouache on cartridge paper
Inscribed *633*
c.1935

SD.2025.1979

492

The *Cactus* chintz
68 × 77·5
Roller-printed cotton
1938

By Lewis Jones for Warner. Note the large early Victorian design in bright colours.

Lent by Warner & Sons Ltd (No.C.7798)

Part Four: 1939–1963

With the outbreak of the Second World War Rex Silver, now 60, began to reduce his staff. By 1943 there were only two full-time members of staff working at the Studio – Frank Price and Lewis Jones, and two outside designers – H.C. Bareham and Madeleine Lawrence.

Most of the Studio's work at this time was for designs based on period subjects. During the 1940s Madeleine Lawrence continued to produce exquisitely coloured naturalistic floral designs for dress fabrics, possibly for Liberty & Co., but the absence of sales records for this period makes it difficult to be certain. Both Lewis Jones and H.C. Bareham produced designs based on simple leaf and grass motifs, and on Scandinavian folk art, with stylized flowers, animals and birds, framed in panels. But throughout this period it was the growing popularity of neo-Baroque, Regency and Early Victorian designs that provided the Silver Studio with most of its work, and enabled Rex Silver to keep the Studio going. What had begun as a smart and sophisticated movement in interior decoration in the early 1930s had become much more widespread by the late 1940s. Wallpaper manufacturers such as John Line, Sanderson and Coles produced 'Regency' stripe wallpapers, and papers with designs of classical motifs and ribbon trellis. For printed textiles the Silver Studio produced a wide range of elaborate designs ranging from panels of scenes from early nineteenth-century sporting prints to copies of flowers from seventeenth-century Dutch still-life paintings, framed in acanthus scroll work. Because Rex Silver had always insisted on a very high standard of draughtsmanship, the production of these designs posed few problems. Frank Price in particular did some superb work in these styles. A number of colour schemes were particularly fashionable, and were based on the juxtaposition of a light colour, such as beige, cream or grey, with a much richer one, such as deep blue, pillar-box red or burgundy.

493

Crown Wallpaper catalogue
18·5 × 18·5
1939

These illustrations are useful to show how wallpaper was used in suburban houses in the 1930s – dull, often embossed, ground papers enlivened by the use of Modernist cut-out borders.

SE.472.1979

494

Design for a woven textile
72·2 × 53·2
Watercolour on detail paper
Inscribed *10736*
1939

This design is typical of those bought by the more design-conscious English manufacturers such as the Edinburgh Weavers, Donald Brothers etc. The simple leaf motif shows the influence of contemporary Scandinavian design.

SD.1483.1979

***495**

Design for a dress silk
16·5 × 16·5
Watercolour, gouache on cartridge paper
Inscribed in pencil *9509*

Note the Scandinavian influence in the use of simple flowers and geometric shapes

SD.1455.1979

496

Glazed chintz, *The Drayton*
96 × 78·5
Roller-printed cotton
1939

Designed by Lewis Jones of the Silver Studio and printed by Stead McAlpin for Warner

Lent by Warner & Sons Ltd (No.C8219)

497

Wallpaper pattern book
37 × 50·8
Inscribed, on cover, *Westminster Wallcoverings*
1940

SW.28.1976

498

Printed linen-*Darius*
Roller-printed linen
1940

Traditional, neo-Jacobean linen by Madeleine Lawrence, printed by Warner in 1940

Lent by Warner & Sons Ltd

***499**

Design for a chintz
27·2 × 23·5
Watercolour on detail paper
Inscribed *12187*
1940

A fashionable Regency revival chintz by G. Turley. Note the typically 1930s predominance of sombre colours.

SD.1451.1979

***500**

Design for a printed cotton
27 × 26·5
Watercolour on detail paper
Inscribed *13071*
1945

An example of a design inspired by mid-European folk art. This type of design became increasingly popular in the 1940s. By Frank Price.

SD.1304.1979

501

Glazed chintz
61 × 97·5
1947

From Silver Studio design No.13480 by Lewis Jones, and manufactured by A.H. Lee. The design is based on scenes from early nineteenth-century sporting prints in a trellis framework of oak leaves.

ST.43.1979

502

Design for a printed linen
27 × 23
Gouache on detail paper
Inscribed *13784*
1948

By Lewis Jones. Old English needlework continued to be a major source of inspiration for furnishing fabrics throughout the 1940s and 1950s.

SD.2041.1979

503

Glazed chintz
81 × 56 (mount size)
1948

Seven colourways of a glazed chintz from a design by Frank Price of the Silver Studio. Although the design is derived from a traditional early nineteenth-century chintz, the colours are typical of those used for smart traditional furnishing textiles in the 1950s.

ST.21.1979

504

An advertisement for A.H. Lee
32·5 × 48
Inscribed *Arthur H. Lee & Sons Inc/Price List for Spring 1949/AHLS/Chintz No.7486*
1949

The background for this advertisement is a chintz designed by Lewis Jones, executed in 1947 and based on scenes from early nineteenth-century sporting prints

SE.531.1979

495

499

500

505

Design for a dress fabric
18 × 15
Watercolour on detail paper
Inscribed *Bulgarian 13899*
1949

European folk art had inspired English textile designers since the Russian Ballet was first performed in London. Harrods had advertised textiles with designs from Hungarian peasant art in the early 1920s and the Stockholm Exhibition of 1930, and the Swedish Art Exhibition of 1931 had encouraged an interest in Scandinavian folk art.

SD.1450.1979

506

Five colourways of a roller-printed cotton
Each sample 21 × 14
c.1950

Produced by Sanderson from a design by H.C.Bareham

ST.30.1979

507

Advertisement for Bevis fabrics
31·5 × 23·5
Inscribed *Bevis/Fabrics/Simpson & Godlee Ltd, Manchester, England*
1950

Advertisement from Silver Studio design No.14105 by Frank Price for Simpson and Godlee

SE.528.1979

***508**

Design for an advertisement for Bevis fabrics
25 × 17·5
Watercolour on detail paper
Inscribed *Bevis/14115*
1950

This design by Lewis Jones was based on a late eighteenth-century silk picture, and typifies the whimsical, rather theatrical approach that characterised middle-class English decorating after the Second World War

SD.405.1978

508

***509**

Trial design for an advertisement for Bevis fabrics
30 × 18·5
Pen and ink and watercolour on detail paper
Inscribed *14240/Bev/Fab*
1950

This design for an advertisement, based on Rex Whistler's illustrations and executed by Lewis Jones, is typical of the vogue for a rather whimsical neo-Regency decoration. This style had begun in the early 1930s, but its popularity with the English middle classes continued for long after the Second World War.

SD.406.1978

510

Printed cotton
71 × 122
1950

By Lewis Jones from Silver Studio design No.14169. Design of cricketing scenes from an early nineteenth-century print.

ST.41.1979

509

511

Printed cotton
81·5 × 60
c.1950

Design by Frank Price based on late eighteenth-century *Toile de Jouy*. Design of groups of musicians and with motifs from classical architecture. Note the fashionable 1950s colour combination of yellow and grey.

ST.50.1979

512

Design for a chintz
89 × 72
Watercolour and pencil on cartridge paper
Inscribed *K2241/14391*
c.1950

By Lewis Jones. In a pamphlet produced by Fortnum and Mason, c.1950, *Fabrics and Their Uses*, the author stated 'Fabrics show today's strong tendency towards Regency and Empire characteristics and the French touch (*Jouy*) of the early 19th century'.

SD.1249.1979

513

Glazed chintz
39·5 × 40
1952

From Silver Studio design No.14514 by Lewis Jones, based on early nineteenth-century sporting prints

ST.42.1977

514

Glazed chintz
200 × 90
Roller-printed cotton
c.1955

From a design by Frank Price based on late eighteenth-century decorative motifs – scrollwork, ribbons, etc., in brown, ochre and white on steel-grey ground

ST.64.1979

515

Design for a chintz
102 × 95
Watercolour on cartridge paper
Inscribed *14864*
1955

By Frank Price from a sketch by Madeleine Lawrence for David Whitehead Fabrics Ltd

SD.2002.1979

***516**

Two designs for printed furnishing textiles
each 35 × 30
Gouache and watercolour on cartridge paper
Inscribed *14885/15064*
c.1955

These two designs were both executed by H.C.Bareham, who was responsible for most of the modern designs of the Silver Studio in the 1950s. Both would have been described at the time as 'Contemporary' – a term which replaced 'Modernist' in the 1950s for describing avant-garde design. The 1950s saw a craze for designs for wallpaper and textiles based on decorative panels. The basis for these two designs are geometric patterns used on panels for motifs from Scandinavian folk art.

SD.441–2.1978

517

Embossed wallpaper
47·5 × 54·5
Distemper on paper
Inscribed, *verso, Sanderson Wallpaper*
c.1955

SW.1325.1978

516

518

Wallpaper
38·2 × 24·3
Distemper on paper
Inscribed, *verso, Line*
c.1955

Neo-Regency paper of design of panels containing musical instruments

SW.1324.1978

519

Embossed wallpaper
46·1 × 40·4
Distemper on paper
Inscribed, *verso, Sanderson Wallpaper/British Made*
c.1950

SW.1134.1977

520

Wallpaper, *The Thurlow*
38 × 24
Distemper on paper
Inscribed, *verso, Line/Thurlow/79082*
c.1950

Block-printed wallpaper of a design that was to become ubiquitous in middle-class homes in the 1950s – The Regency Stripe

SW.1125.1979

516

The following designs (521–3) are all by Frank Price, in fashionable neo-eighteenth- and early nineteenth-century styles. The Silver Studio ended where it had begun, in the production of exquisitely drawn period designs.

521

Design for a printed furnishing textile
49 × 34·5
Gouache on detail paper
Inscribed *15470*
1960

SD.1392.1979

***522**

Design for a chintz
66 × 41
Watercolour on cartridge paper
Inscribed *15663A*
1962

SD.1550.1979

523

Design for a chintz
71·5 × 48
Watercolour on detail paper
Inscribed *15644A*
1962

For David Whitehead Fabrics Ltd

SD.2027.1979

Silver Studio Designers

This is an incomplete list of designers who worked for the Silver Studio. In many cases it has not been possible to find out more than when they actually worked at the Studio. The author would be very pleased to hear from anyone who could supply further information on the designers listed below.

522

Stacy Aumonier
b.1877, d.1929

The son of William Aumonier, a well-known nineteenth-century architectural sculptor. He began his career as an apprentice in the Silver Studio c.1895 but left in 1898. Became a well-known novelist and writer of short stories. He was related to Frederic Aumonier, Director of William Woollams Wallpapers, and cousin to Louise Aumonier, who also worked for the Silver Studio. His nephew, Eric Stacy Aumonier (b.1899) executed the 'Empire' panels for the *Daily Express* building in Fleet Street, c.1930.

H.C.Bareham

Trained at Leyton and Hammersmith Schools of Art and worked at the Silver Studio from 1903 until 1915. After the First World War he became a free-lance designer, producing both period and, after 1930, simple, elegant Modernist designs such as the *Quaking Grass* brocade produced by Walter Franklin and illustrated in *British Textile Designers of Today* by H.G.Hayes Marshall, 1939, p.63

In 1943 he returned to working for the Silver Studio as an outside designer, working at home. This arrangement continued until the close of the Studio in 1963.

E.V.Borton

Worked in the Silver Studio from 1910 until 1915, having previously studied at Hammersmith and Chelsea Schools of Art, and the Central School of Arts and Crafts. He worked on period designs whilst at the Silver Studio, but later became well-known for his elegant and original designs for woven fabrics in the 1930s, when he supplied designs to Morton Sundour and Donald Bros Ltd (see H.G.Hayes Marshall: *British Textile Designers Today*, 1939, p.83).

John Churton

Worked at the Silver Studio in 1934 but unfortunately contracted tuberculosis. Produced some of the Studio's best avant-garde work of the 1930s, mostly for woven textiles and carpets.

Herbert J.Crofts
d.1937

Worked at the Silver Studio from c.1900 to 1937, and acted as chief designer after Harry Silver left the Studio in 1916. Specialised in elegantly drawn historic designs for textiles, making a speciality of adapting late eighteenth-century chinoiserie patterns for commercial manufacture.

J.R.Houghton

Chief designer for the Silver Studio after Harry Napper, from 1898 to 1901. Seems to have left the Silver Studio shortly afterwards and opened a studio of his own at Little Euston, Dunmow, Essex. Continued to sell designs through the Studio, invariably elaborate imitations of late eighteenth-century chinoiserie patterns.

W.A.Hughes

Worked full-time for the Silver Studio from c.1900 until 1915, thereafter until 1926 appears to have worked either part-time, or used the Silver Studio as an agency for the sale of his designs. He was one of the first designers working for the Studio to use brilliant *Ballet Russe* colours (around 1913–14) and he avoided working in historical styles, producing exotic, fashionable, Oriental or abstract patterns.

Lewis Jones
d.1953

Worked at the Silver Studio from c.1910 until 1953. An extremely versatile designer, but was best at producing period designs for textiles and wallpapers. Rex Silver was on the point of offering him a partnership with Frank Price when he died.

John Illingworth Kay
b.1870, d.1950

Born in Kirkaldy, Fifeshire and educated at the High School there. He came to London c.1890 and was certainly working at the Silver Studio by 1892. With Harry Napper, he was one of the two best designers working in the Silver Studio. Won a prize for a cover design for *The Studio* magazine in 1893, and would have won first prize if his lettering had been a little better.* Very interested in designing for book covers, and probably was responsible for a number of book covers for Blackie executed by the Studio in 1898. Actively involved in the Studio's Silver Stencils for Rottmann & Co. Left the studio in 1900 to manage the stencilling department of Essex Wallpapers. Left Essex Wallpapers 1922, and taught part-time at the Central School of Arts and Crafts. Worked as a free-lance designer, selling to Morton Sundour, Grafton and Liberty. Great friend of Harry Napper and Lindsay Butterfield. Member of the Art Workers' Guild and keen amateur watercolourist, exhibiting at the Royal Academy.

*Letter from Gleeson White to J.Illingworth Kay, 16 August 1893:
'The letter was not . . . sufficiently exact for reproduction . . . or in styles equal to the ornamental work, which they considered so extremely good that it was a genuine regret they found themselves bound by the terms of the rules to exclude them from the first and second places.'

G.R.Kingbourne

Worked at the Silver Studio from 1919 until 1924. Specialised in brilliantly coloured designs based on Japanese landscapes – pine-trees, magnolias, exotic birds, etc.

Archibald Knox
b.1864, d.1933

Seems to have worked part-time at the Silver Studio in 1898 and produced the earliest designs for Liberty's *Cymric* Silver. He used the Silver Studio as an agency for the sale of some of his pattern designs for textiles etc., at least until his return to London in 1904 and possibly later.

Madeleine C.Lawrence
d.1952

Worked for the Silver Studio from 1918 until 1949, and, like Winifred Mold, worked at home. She produced some excellent chinoiserie and Modernist designs in the 1920s, and 1930s, and was responsible for many of the floral designs for Liberty dress fabrics in the 1930s. Rex Silver wrote on her memorial card 'One very gifted artist who worked on some of the Silver Studio designs in her own home'.

Winifred Mold
b.1894

Trained at the Art Department of the Paddington Technical Institute, and joined the staff of the Silver Studio in 1912, but always worked at home. Herbert Crofts, the head designer during Miss Mold's period at the Studio encouraged her to work away from the Studio to prevent her being influenced by the other staff. Specialised in soft, abstract dress fabrics and elaborate period designs for furnishing textiles. Left the Studio in 1935 to look after her parents.

Harry Napper
d.1930

Came to work for the Silver Studio c.1893 and stayed until 1898. He managed the design production of the Studio after Arthur Silver's death in 1896. He continued to use the Silver Studio as an agency for the sale of his designs up until his death. Produced some of the Silver Studio's best Art Nouveau pattern designs in the 1890s, and was also a talented designer of furniture and metalwork, as can be seen from illustrations in the catalogue *Officers' Ideal Quarters* produced by Norman and Stacey Ltd, in 1902. Like Archibald Knox and John Illingworth Kay, he was an enthusiastic watercolourist, and some of his paintings are included in the exhibition. Examples of his textile designs are illustrated in the Victoria and Albert Museum Catalogue of *The Liberty Centenary Exhibition*, 1975.

Edwin Parker

Worked for the Silver Studio from 1920 until 1941. Whilst being particularly good at period styles, he also produced some imaginative Modernist designs for dress and furnishing fabrics in the 1930s.

Roy Passano

Worked at the Silver Studio from 1937 until 1939, producing Modernist designs for textiles.

Frank Price

Apart from Archibald Knox, Frank Price was undoubtedly the best draughtsman to have worked in the Silver Studio. This is partly explained by his early training in an architect's office. He subsequently worked in the design studio of Gaudioz and Fauser Ltd (c.1907), and then for Albert Griffiths. He began his work for the Silver Studio in December 1922. He left to work with a former Silver Studio designer G.R.Kingbourne in 1935, thence to Sanderson as chief designer until Sanderson were bombed out in 1940. He returned to the Silver Studio in 1941 and stayed until the Studio closed in 1963. From 1953 onwards he was the sole designer working in the Silver Studio, and spent most of his time producing exquisitely drawn designs for printed textiles from late eighteenth-century and early nineteenth-century sources.

Louis Silas

An artist friend of Arthur Silver who designed a few neo-Baroque wallpapers for the studio in the 1890s, and produced some theatrical romantic landscape designs for Rex to adapt for cretonnes in the 1920s and early 1930s.

Harry Silver
b.1882, d.1972

Harry Silver supervised the design production of the Silver Studio from 1901 to 1916, when he left to join the Army. Influenced by Archibald Knox's work, and frequently used Celtic motifs in his patterns. Executed designs for Liberty *Cymric* Silver after 1906. Particularly good at economical, highly stylized late Art Nouveau designs, and produced some textile designs in 1915 influenced by contemporary French designers.

George H.Willis

Worked at the Silver Studio from 1916 up until the early 1930s, when he left to open up his own studio at 12a, The Mall, Ealing, W5. He had trained at Regent Street Polytechnic. He specialised in period designs whilst working at the Studio and, like Frank Price, was extremely good at reproducing classical styles.